CUT NOSE
Who Stands on a Cloud

To Arlene & Dennis —

Thanks for your interest

in my book.

Loren Dean Boutin

Cut Nose

CUT NOSE
Who Stands on a Cloud

Loren Dean Boutin

NORTH STAR PRESS OF ST. CLOUD, INC.
St. Cloud, Minnesota

ISBN: 0-87839-236-X

First Edition, June 2006

Printed in the United States of America
by Versa Press, Inc., East Peoria, Illinois

Published by North Star Press of St. Cloud, Inc.
P.O. Box 451
St. Cloud, Minnesota 56302
northstarpress.com
nspress@cloudnet.com

Dedication

To Reconciliation

ॐ ✦ ॐ

Acknowledgements

I HARDLY KNOW HOW TO THANK all the people who contributed to this book with their support and encouragement. There were many, but outstanding among them was my soulmate, Beverly, who was my main editor and who tolerated my expenditures of time and the many resources that went into the production of this book.

I also thank my readers, Ed Red Owl, Bud Lawrence, Sharynn Baker, Jerry Fogel, and some of my family, especially my sister Cheryl Elfrink and nephew Chad Elfrink, all of whom gave much needed encouragement and support.

I am grateful to John Koblas for his comments.

Special thanks to Elden Lawrence, Professor of Cultural Studies at Mankato State University, who edited my book for cultural correctness and who offered many constructive suggestions for improvement.

I thank Corinne Dwyer and the North Star Press publishing company in St. Cloud, Minnesota, for being willing to take a chance on my first book.

Lastly, for their patience, I want to thank all the interested people who kept asking, year after year, "How's the book coming?" Well, finally, here it it.

ℑ ✦ ℜ

Contents

Foreword

FOR A VERY LONG TIME, only a few people have been talking about how the good Doctor W.W. Mayo, the father of the famous Mayo brothers, took the body of Cut Nose from the grave after the simultaneous hanging of thirty-eight Indians in 1862. Most people in the area of Mankato, Minnesota, where the hanging took place, don't know very much about that, and a surprising number don't even know about the hanging, much less the grave robbery.

The first time I heard about this grave robbery was on a local radio station. A news commentator was expressing some astonishment at the story, and that got my attention. But then I didn't hear anything more about it for quite some time. It seemed as if the local community suppressed this story as though it should not be talked about at all. Still, the story stuck in my mind for a long time (several years). Whenever I came across anything relevant to the few bits of information I knew about it, my base of information would grow and my interest grew with it.

The more I learned about this brief period of history, when there was a local war between the indigenous Indians and the invading white settlers, the more interesting it became. For a while, the story seemed to become more absurd and incredible with each new bit of information. When I began to look into the historical accounts of these events more earnestly, reading all I could find in the local library, I was astonished to find many of the "absurdities" verified. The old axiom that "truth is stranger than fiction" is vividly realized in this history.

This book is based upon facts and historical events that actually occurred, but those facts are limited to the few details that were recorded by highly prejudiced reporters of the events associated with the war between Indians and whites in 1862. Facts that were reported reflected the biased perspectives of the whites, who were the only reporters. Many of the principal Indians involved in the conflict were killed and, therefore, obviously incapable of recording their points of view for posterity.

Furthermore, very few Indians at the time had any literary skills. Consequently, any existing report of the point of view of the Indians at the time was almost assuredly recorded by whites and subject to distortion from racial prejudices and many other possible influences. To add to all of the confusion over what actually did happen, one can find widely divergent reports of a single event from different eyewitnesses. Who is to be believed? In some cases there is little agreement about what actually happened and the possibility exists that none of the reports of what happened are wholly accurate.

A professor of mass communications at a local university, Charles Lewis, studied the content of newspaper articles that were published about the events reported in this book. He described them as graphic, bigoted, mocking, and celebrating the murder of Indians. During a lecture on this subject (at Mankato State University, April 12, 2004) he said, "I can't think of one Minnesota paper that I'm aware of that had much sympathy [for the Indians]." To the contrary, extermination of the Indians was openly advocated. The professor described a secret society called "The Knights of the Forest" formed specifically for the purpose of pressuring the government to remove the Indians from southern Minnesota. The professor speculated that the editors of the local newspapers might have been members.

When gathering information for this book, I did make a diligent effort to find whatever pertinent facts existed in the present day records of the events of 1862. Historical accounts of those events include some excellently detailed descriptions of many things that happened, including verbatim reprints of relevant written communications, quotations of things people said, and names and dates that help to put in chronological sequence the course of the events that occurred. But the "facts" must be presumed to have been altered by the various reporters to some extent, and the reporters were almost always white. The old expression, "little white lies" acquires new meaning when one reads some of the reports from the time with a skeptical eye. In those reports, little effort was made to hide or apologize for the widely held attitudes among whites that the Indians were sub-human savages, uncivilized, merciless, brutal, never to be trusted, and impossible to civilize. How can one trust the "facts" reported by people with such attitudes?

Had there been more reports of the Indians' perspectives on the events that occurred in 1862 this writer's work would have been made much easier. With the few reports that exist, however, it was often left to the writer to deduce what the Indians' perspectives might have been. No doubt there will be many readers who will question how the writer could presume to do this, but whether or not the effort was presumptive, it was necessary. Otherwise this book could not have been written.

To write this book, it was essential for the writer to read between the lines of reported history in most instances when all available data regarding a given event came from a white man's book. Also, the book describes many events which have never been previously described anywhere. These events are merely the author's interpolations between events known to have occurred and what logically must have happened or likely happened in order for the known events to have occurred as they did.

The writer has taken some liberty in reporting dialogue that is part of this story. Most of the Dakotah people of the time could speak little English. The white immigrants could speak little of the Dakotah language. Communication between the Dakotah and the whites began with mere gestures. Verbal communication developed after a time as each group became more familiar with the other's language. Verbal communication was difficult between the Indians and whites throughout the story's time period. The author chose to circumvent the confusion inherent in such communication difficulties by simply reporting all dialogue in English, not that there was much choice, as the author is not fluent in the Dakotah language and few readers would have any exposure to it. In reality, almost all the dialogue between one Indian and another would have been in the Dakotah language, and dialogue between an Indian and a white person would have been very difficult in most cases.

Chapter One

෨ ✦ ଔ

The World of Cut Nose
as a Youth

T HIS IS A BOOK ABOUT A DAKOTAH INDIAN warrior named
Mapeokinijin. In the Dakotah language, this name means, "Who
Stands On a Cloud." He was also known more popularly as "Cut
Nose." He was an outstanding Dakotah warrior and was among the thirty-
eight warriors who were hanged together in Mankato, Minnesota, in 1862 in
the single largest simultaneous execution ever to take place in American history. Dr. William Worrell Mayo stole his body from the grave less than twenty-four hours after the bodies were buried. He took the body home, dissect-
ed it, and kept the bones in a large cast iron kettle in his office. Dr. Mayo's
sons, the famous Mayo brothers, learned their osteology from these bones.[1]

This story is about how Cut Nose grew up, how he lived his life, and
how he died. It is also about the land of the Indians before the arrival of the
white man, the changes that took place when the white man arrived, and the
Indians learning about the white man's ways, white man's tools, and white
man's alcohol.

The story also briefly describes the conflict that developed between
the Indians and the white man as, ruthlessly, the white man began to push
the local Indians farther west, just as they had pushed the Indians out of the
East. The story describes a time when the Dakotah Indians were totally

evicted from Minnesota, exiled to less desirable places, shipped like animals to such places, or outlawed and killed on sight.

Even before the white man arrived in Minnesota, life was not very idyllic for the people who were already there. There had been times when life was better, but the people of those times left little record of that. The white man's arrival caused fighting among the native people themselves even before the white man arrived in the state. Long before the white man began arriving in Minnesota, large white communities were already well established in the East. They were pushing Indians out of that area to live elsewhere. Where were those Indians to go but into the frontiers of the West and into the territories of some other Indians? When they did that, they caused trouble. Those poor people were in a very pitiable situation with whites evicting them from their homelands and other Indians reluctant to roll out the welcome mat in new territories. These circumstances were so desperate at times that the local Indian people, mainly the Dakotah and the Ojibwa, killed each other over them.

So it was in Minnesota in the year 1820, the approximate time when Mapeokinijin was born. Whites had settled the eastern seaboard of the continent, pushing the Indians west in a domino effect, causing fighting among displaced and indigenous Indians all along the way. In Minnesota, Indians from the East were trying to move in, disrupting the balance of peace long before the white man ever showed up. Minnesota was a battleground for a war between the nomadic hunting Indians of the plains, the Dakotah, also known as the Sioux,[2] and the displaced Indians from the East, the Ojibwa, also known as Chippewa (a phonetic distortion), who were mostly farmers and gatherers. Mapeokinijin, a Dakotah, was born into this world of strife and conflict, never to know real peace in his lifetime. Ultimately, he would die at the end of a rope, hanged by white men as a war criminal.

Even before he was born, Mapeokinijin had little chance for a very long life. There were extreme hazards to be overcome from the time of his conception. Life was hard for the Dakotah even when times were good. But in bad times, food might be scarce, the weather could be deadly fierce, and bearing a child to full term was sometimes very difficult for a Dakotah woman. The birthing of a child was hazardous, the only assistance being the practiced but unskilled help of other women. And sometimes, a Dakotah woman would simply go off into the woods by herself to deliver her baby, returning with the child in her arms when the birthing was all over.

As a baby, hazards included the occasional attacks of Ojibwa warriors who would sometimes show up when all the men of the tribe were gone away on a hunting trip. The Ojibwa would kill all of the Dakotah women and children they could find. The women and children would hide, of course, when they saw or were warned of the Ojibwa approaching. A crying child, however, would enable the Ojibwa warriors to find and kill them.

It is told that a Dakotah mother would smother a crying child in these circumstances to avoid detection.[3] She would hold the child's nose and cover its mouth with her hand to stop it from crying so that their hiding place would not be revealed by the sound. The child would lose consciousness, of course, and then the mother would let it breathe again. Children learned not to cry. It is possible that this is how Dakotah people learned the stoicism for which they became known.

Even today it is somewhat rare to see a Dakotah child cry, although the Dakotah people are no longer subjected to the same threats as in the old days, and Dakotah mothers no longer smother their children. Perhaps some form of Darwinian natural selection took place—babies who cried were killed by an enemy, and only those who didn't cry grew up to reproduce. It is doubtful that the practice of smothering lasted long enough for that to happen, but who knows?

When Cut Nose was still a toddler, much of his play activity was devoted to developing and acquiring the skills necessary to be a warrior. In generations past, the play was different in subtle ways, more of it devoted to becoming a hunter, developing skills for survival in the wilderness that was home. Some of the hunting activities overlapped with fighting activities, of course. Even warriors need to survive. For the most part, the hunters of a tribe were also the warriors of the tribe. The arrow that would kill a deer was the same one that would kill a man. Learning to shoot the arrow accurately was acquiring a skill that would serve both purposes. Stalking or laying an ambush for a deer was like stalking or laying an ambush for an enemy warrior—many of the same skills were utilized. Planning a strategy, approaching the quarry cautiously and noiselessly, staying downwind to conceal noises and smells, hiding in the grass or using whatever cover was available for concealment, approaching silently and only when not being observed, observing but not being observed—these were the skills involved.

With the new necessity of having to defend one's homeland from being taken over by newcomers, however, Mapeokinijin practiced his hunting skills with targets that resembled human beings as often as they resembled game animals. Many times he rehearsed in his mind how he would kill men in combat, what weapon he would use in this situation and what weapon in that one, and there would be discussion among the children regarding the relative merits of one weapon over another in a given situation.

Disputes were settled by consultation with the elders of the tribe who would pass on to the children the wisdom they had acquired through their experience and from what they had learned from their elders. It was common to see a group of children listening intently to an elder telling them stories of the past. Often, these stories involved warfare.

Children could often be seen at play engaged in mock hand-to-hand mortal combat. Through this play they became very skillful at lunging, thrusting, parrying, dodging, blocking, or otherwise attacking each other or defending themselves. They also learned to attack with sticks, clubs, lances, knives, and other fencing weapons. They knew relatively little about guns. A few of the Indians had guns, having acquired them from the traders in exchange for furs, but the traditional weapons—knives, lances, and bows and arrows—were still the arms of the children and young men preparing in their play to become hunters and warriors. The guns were reserved for the most skillful of warriors.

Verbal instruction from the elders gave the children certain attitudes about the world around them, about hunting, fighting, what was right, and what was wrong according to ancient cultural customs and traditions. The closest thing the children had to formal education was the storytelling and instruction provided by the older men who no longer accompanied the younger men on hunting expeditions or in war parties. They sat with the children by a fire and passed on to them all the things they had learned during their long lives, the lore and culture and customs of their tribe. They described the methods and techniques of hunting and fighting that had been most successful for them in their battles and adventures of the past.

The boys got one kind of education, and the girls received another. Girls learned the tasks and chores typical for women. They watched their mothers and their older sisters, learning that the women deferred to the men in most important matters. Among other things, women had babies and cared for the children. They also gathered wood, built the morning fires, cleaned and cooked the game brought home by the men. They preserved the game that was not eaten immediately, and they tanned hides and made clothing and robes from them. They fetched the water needed for cooking and drinking and washing. All of this was hard work. Although the location of an Indian camp was usually selected for its proximity to water, sometimes the only place to get water was still quite far away.

Young girls learned that a woman should become skillful in making the most of whatever food was available. Women needed to know how to find herbs and spices in the woods and on the prairies to make the food taste better. They needed to know what plants these things came from, how to recognize them, and where they could be found. They needed to know about mushrooms (especially about avoiding the poisonous ones), and all the edible roots, nuts, fruits, and berries. They harvested these things as they became available. The season for some of these foods was very short so they learned how to preserve these foods by washing them and drying them in the sun. Dried fruits and berries and vegetables would remain edible for a long time.

Meat was a very large part of the diet of the Dakotah people, and when game was plentiful, everyone ate until they were full. The meat was cooked over an open fire. One fresh buffalo could provide enough meat for a whole village for many days. Any surplus of meat would spoil very soon unless preserved in some manner. In winter, the meat could be frozen in a cache out doors, so preserving the meat in that season was no problem. For a large part of the year, however, there were no freezing temperatures, and something else had to be done. When temperatures were warm, the meat would be cut into thin strips and smoked over an open fire or dried in the sun. This treatment would make the meat into "jerky" or "pemican." Smoking or drying the meat in this manner could preserve the meat for months.

Preserved meat would enable the Dakotah to survive long periods when game was scarce, and it was a way of preventing waste when food was in abundance. The Dakotah had respect for the herds of animals on which they depended for sustenance. They took only as much game as they needed, recognizing that the best way to preserve their food source was to let the animals live on to be available when needed in the future. If one buffalo was needed for a village and the hunters brought in two of them, then one would have to be preserved. There were always strips of meat hanging over the fire of every lodge in the village. Seldom was any part of an animal wasted. The skins were highly valued and used for a variety of purposes. Strips of sinew were used for bindings. Even the bones of an animal were used to make good soup, then used for tools.

Women helped to make the weapons used in hunting. They made arrows and arrowheads. They learned to split feathers to make fletchings for the arrows. They learned how to attach the fletchings so the arrow would spin in flight, making it fly straight and true. They learned what sticks to select and gather for making the shafts of the arrows, and how to straighten and dry the sticks over a fire. They learned how to select the right stones for arrowheads, and how to chip flakes from the stones to shape them and make a fine point and sharp edge on them. And they learned how to lash the arrowheads to the shaft with strips of sinew when the process reached the final stage. For many reasons, the hunter who would use the arrow would mark it with his own personal special mark to identify it as his.

Women were not expected to participate in the hunting and did not become skilled with hunting weapons, but the things they were required to do involved a lot of work with knives, so they became very skillful with the use of a knife. They skinned game, butchered game, cut the meat into strips for making jerky, processed furs, and made clothing. A knife was an essential tool for their activities. Most women either carried a sharp knife on their person or had one available within reach almost always.

Equally as important as learning how to be a good cook was learning how a woman could be attractive to men and how a woman should behave, especially around men. Boys learned the subtleties of how to treat women with respect while at the same time keeping them in their place. They stopped playing together at a relatively young age partly because of these influences and also because their usual activities kept them apart.

Girls wore dresses. Boys wore breechclouts and leggings. One reason the girls were not available to the boys was that, while the girls were still quite young, they became sexually active. Then the older men, the braves and elders, would become very possessive of the young girls. The older men did not want the boys fooling around with them, and they would severely punish any boy caught doing so. The girls would sometimes marry the older men at the very brink of puberty, and on rare occasions, even before puberty. Boys of nine, ten, or eleven years of age were considered to be children, but many girls of those ages were considered to be women if they were precocious in their physical development. They were even considered to be the most attractive and desirable of all women when they were young, and fresh, and new, and sweet, and innocent, and tender. And they were passionate, loving, appreciative, impressionable, and exceptionally devoted to their first lover. What man would not want such a woman? Many of the older men wanted three or four. Polygamy was a common practice.

Indian boys were not very different from white boys when it came to play activities, except they had to take play more seriously. White boys played for fun to a much greater extent than Indian boys, not that the Indian boys didn't have fun. For the young warriors, however, the play also had a quality of practice that was not present in the same measure in the play activities of the white children. In their play, the Indian boys were developing new skills or sharpening their abilities in the skills they already possessed. They were preparing for the inevitable day when the success of a hunt or the outcome of close combat with a mortal enemy would depend upon their proficiency in these skills.

In their play, the Indian boys would emulate the models of behavior presented by their elders to some extent, but the learning involved in developing some of these skills was shaped by naturally occurring events as well. For example, there were many opportunities to practice the skill of stalking, quietly approaching a game animal, sneaking up on it to get a close shot at it, a shot close enough that it would be effectively lethal rather than one that would just superficially wound the animal. If a wounded animal could escape, it likely would go off somewhere to hide and die and be wasted. Indians depended on game for their sustenance and survival so it was especially important that game animals should not be wasted. It was necessary to get close enough to a game animal to kill it. Obviously, stalking was a skill that was essential and much more important to Indians than to whites.

Few of the Indians had guns, as a rule, and the weapons that they did have were not very effective at long range. Until the white man came to the area, guns were not available to the Indians. Even after the white man arrived with his guns the Indians could rarely obtain them. Indians were not trusted with them because the whites didn't trust the Indians to use them for just hunting game. Obviously, if a gun can be used to kill a deer at a range of 100 yards or more, a man could be killed at the same distance. The whites enjoyed the advantage that guns gave them and they did not wish to give that up by allowing the Indians to have guns also.

The weapons that the Indians did have were relatively primitive and required the user to be close to the target to be effective. They had bows and arrows, and these were their best long distance weapons, but even these weapons were not well developed. Europeans had better archery equipment, but this didn't matter because even the best archery equipment was relatively ineffective compared with guns.

The Indians typically would make their own weapons, including their own bows and arrows. It took some training and skill to make these weapons. There were a variety of trees in the forest and therefore varieties of wood for the making of weapons. The elders taught the children how to select the best wood for making bows, what wood was best for the shafts of arrows, what wood was best for the handles of tomahawks, what was best for lances and spears.

Women participated in the making of weapons, but they were not expected to develop exceptional skills with using the weapons. Women did get to be very proficient with knives because they used them a lot in their daily activities and almost always had one of their own, but they seldom used their knives as weapons. Women did most of the cooking and used knives to prepare game and other ingredients for the meals. They also used their knives as tools in the manufacture of other weapons for the men. Women could use axes, too, because they made the cook fires. They gathered and chopped wood for the fires.

The manufacture of weapons was a constant activity that took up a lot of the time of the women and children and older people while the men were out hunting. The old folks taught the young folks how to do it. It was a continuously necessary activity because the hunters used up a lot of arrows. Arrows were like ammunition. When shot at game animals they commonly would be broken or lost, especially when the shot failed to hit the target.

Arrows that went sailing past the target and flying through the woods were seldom retrieved. They could be used again if they didn't break and if they could be found, but they were hard to find, usually, and often as not they were imbedded in a tree or buried under grass and impossible to find. Often the hunters didn't bother to look for expended arrows. Thousands of arrows were lost. Lost arrows had to be replaced with new ones. As a consequence, it is still possible to find arrowheads in places where the Indians frequently hunted. The arrow itself, the feathers used as fletchings, the cords that bound the arrowhead to the shaft—all these have long ago turned to dust. But the stone arrowheads have endured for many centuries, sometimes looking like new when they are recovered.

Archery requires practice to develop the skill and continued practice to maintain the skill at a given level. The best hunters were constantly trying to improve their skills. The hunters would construct practice ranges where they could have contests. Everyone would attend, either to participate or, as a spectator, to root and cheer for their favorite contestant. In practice, the men could try out new equipment. The best arrows were those that had been tried and found to be true, those that would fly straight when they were shot. If the arrow itself was not straight, or if the flint point was tied on crooked, or if the feather fletchings were faulty, then the arrow might curve away from the target when shot, or it might wobble excessively in flight, slowing it down undesirably. A good arrow would fly straight and true and not break when it struck a bag packed tightly with grass. The arrows that did fly straight were recovered and saved, if possible, and great value was placed upon them. They were the ones to be used in the next hunt or in the next battle.

New bowstrings needed to be tried before they could be trusted. The bows themselves were all different, each having its own peculiar qualities. The hunter had to become intimately familiar with his bow before actually hunting with it. Practice sessions and frequent contests and even more frequent hunting excursions used up a lot of arrows and other equipment that required replacement. So the people who did not go hunting were kept busy with the support services the hunters required.

Stalking is a skill that has obvious important applications on a hunt or perhaps even more importance in the field of combat with any kind of enemy. If a warrior could get within arms reach of an enemy warrior without the enemy even knowing that he is there, that would be the best of circumstances. His chances of killing the enemy then would be very greatly enhanced.

White men thought this kind of behavior was sneaky and somehow unfair. They didn't seem to recognize how unfair it was to shoot an Indian at 100 yards, a range at which the Indian had little chance to fight back. On the other hand, if an Indian were to lie in ambush of a white man or try to sneak up on one, that was thought to be savage, uncivilized, vicious, just plain bad. White men didn't do that kind of thing, or if they did do it, they didn't do it nearly as well. Some Indians were legendary with regard to their ability to sneak up on an enemy.

Stalking and ambushing are the things the Indians did to stay alive. They also did these things to win battles with their enemies. These things were necessary because they had no weapons that were effective at long range. It was necessary to do these things well. So the children were given instruction about these skills and started to practice these skills as soon as they could understand them. The playtime activities of the children often involved stalking and ambushing each other prior to engaging in mock hand-to-hand combat. Hide and seek is a game played by white children in which these skills are used, but the Indians placed more importance on such skills and developed them to perfection.

The best practice for young Indian boys was the actual pursuit of small game in areas near the village. Usually the village would be encamped in a low area near a creek with woods all around. This kind of area would have many advantages over camping out on the plains. Obviously, the creek would provide water for cooking, bathing, washing things, and for watering the animals. There would be plentiful wood for campfires nearby, and there would be many campfires burning almost all the time.

Anytime the boys would leave the village to go into the woods they practiced stalking. Even at the edge of the village there could be game animals. Even when they were not hunting them the boys would be challenged to see if they could get close to the animals before spooking them. The boys learned to recognize all the animals, to know their habits, and to know how to get close to them. They even learned how to talk to them, to imitate the sounds that the animals would make, to lure them to come closer as the boys would lie in ambush.

For example, if a boy in the woods saw a fox approaching, the boy might stand very still and make a sound like a plaintive mouse to attract the fox. A mouse in some kind of trouble and squealing might be just what the fox had been looking for to satisfy his hunger. Hearing the boy's imitation could cause the fox to pause, perk up his ears to listen more closely, and search his field of vision for the source of the sound. It could become a good game to see how close the boy could lure the fox before the fox would get onto the ruse and run away. Sometimes they could lure a fox to within ten feet before the fox would get wise and run away. At a distance of ten feet, a fox could easily be killed with a bow and arrow.

As young boys grew older they would be permitted to venture farther into the woods and to hunt the small game if their skills were adequate. Rabbits, squirrels, and various small birds were plentiful. The boys would feel a special pride if they were able to provide enough for a meal. They would bring home whatever they could get. If it was not enough they might be sent back to try for more. One small squirrel was not enough for a stew, but if they could get one more, or a rabbit, then there would be enough. Nothing would be wasted. One small squirrel might be given to another family that had another small squirrel so they could make a stew. The other family would return the favor on another occasion. In any case, the game would be cooked and eaten or preserved and not wasted.

The boys would go out alone into the woods when they got older, sometimes staying out in the woods for several days at a time if they didn't have any good hunting luck right away. They would come back to the village and tell stories about their adventures in the woods. A boy might boast about how he followed a big buck deer everywhere the deer went for two days, and how at one point he was close enough to have touched the deer as it stood with its head lowered to drink water from the creek a full day's walk downstream. Nobody would doubt his story. The Indians were not given to exaggeration. The truth and accurate descriptions of events were so important to their survival that falsehoods and deceptions were received with severe negative social sanctions. Liars were considered to be absolutely worthless people.

Lone hunters returning to the village with a full bag of freshly killed game were cause for some celebration, especially if their bag was full enough for everyone. There would be a feast because most of the game would have to be eaten so that it would not be wasted, and it was difficult to keep the game fresh or edible for a very long period of time, except in winter. The game that existed in the area was plentiful. There were a variety of game birds including ducks and geese, partridge, prairie chickens, and grouse, to name a few. Some of these were present all year round, but some migrated to warmer climes for the winter. Deer were the most common large game animal, but there would be occasional herds of buffaloes in the area. There were even a few elk around. There also were occasional bears of the black bear species. The buffaloes, being grazing animals, were much more plentiful on the vast grassy plains farther west. There were, without exaggeration, tens of millions of buffaloes there. It is estimated that there may have been as many as fifty million of them scattered across the wide western plains.

The Minnesota River had plenty of fish in it, but the Dakotah preferred game birds and meat. There was even better fishing in the many lakes in the area and the Dakotah did harvest a lot of fish, especially when other game was scarce, but those times of scarcity were rare. Fish was good for some variety in the diet and good for satisfying hunger in hard times, but fish was not considered the best of game. Many fish were bony. Fish skins were almost useless. In contrast, the skins of large game animals provided the material for clothes, bedding, and shelter. The buffaloes, especially, were so useful and so highly valued as to be considered sacred animals.

Meeting an enemy in the woods and having it out with him frequently involved hand-to-hand mortal combat. A typical encounter between two warriors might involve failed attempts to kill each other at a distance and then a continuing fight at close quarters with knives or clubs or whatever was handy. The combatants might end up wrestling around on the ground while attacking each other and trying to defend themselves until one of them would get the best of the other. Both would likely be injured in the struggle, but one of them most likely would be killed.

Aside from practice with weapons and stalking skills, the play activities of children also involved wrestling. They wrestled competitively to hone their skills in anticipation for the day when an enemy warrior might challenge them, and also to establish a level of respect for themselves. The boy who could best another in a wrestling match was socially dominant over the boy who was defeated. Being the most skillful at any of the hunting or fighting activities demanded respect from all the others. Cut Nose was, perhaps, not the absolute best at anything, but he was an athletic and determined competitor who usually came close to being the winner in every contest if, in fact, he did not win it himself.

Cut Nose acquired his name when he was playing with a group of boys from his own village. He was already quite highly respected among his friends for his hunting and fighting skills. He had bested most of his friends at one time or another in wrestling contests. One boy stood apart from the others, however, in that he rarely participated in these events. He attended them sometimes, but usually as a spectator only. He seemed to find amusement in watching the others fight. This was John Otherday, a strong muscular boy who was athletic in many ways, a fast runner, and a hard worker when something needed to be done.

Cut Nose saw Otherday chuckle after another boy had thrown Cut Nose to the ground in a mock battle. A bit embarrassed about having been thrown, Cut Nose was quite annoyed by Otherday's amusement and immediately challenged Otherday to wrestle.

"Do you think this is funny? Come and fight me, you coward," he shouted with an obviously angry tone.

Otherday backed off just a little, saying, "I don't want to fight you. I just thought it was funny the way you landed on your face in the dirt like that. I meant no offense." But the expression on Otherday's face was clearly one of suppressed amusement. He was stifling his continuing laughter. This enraged Cut Nose. Few people today realize just how dangerous it was in the old days to rile an Indian. If an Indian was provoked enough to strike out at a person, he was mad enough to kill that person. In Dakotah traditional law, the cause of a killing was more important than the killing itself. If a murder was the result of provocation, the killer might not be punished at all.

Cut Nose went after Otherday, gave him a vicious shove, and said, "It offends me that you are even here when you will not fight."

Otherday shoved back and the fight was on. Cut Nose threw Otherday to the ground, straddled him, and hit him several times in the face.

Well, this made Otherday mad. He threw Cut Nose off almost effortlessly and quickly made it to his feet. Cut Nose also was on his feet at once and the two of them boxed each other furiously for awhile. Then Otherday managed to throw Cut Nose to the ground, almost exactly like he had been thrown before, face first, and Otherday started to laugh again.

Now Cut Nose went crazy. He drew his knife and made it clear that he intended to kill Otherday, who desperately dodged and avoided several slashes and thrusts. Defensively, he grabbed onto Cut Nose, got hold of his wrist and shook the knife loose. But with his free hand, Cut Nose got a choking hold on Otherday's throat. They were face to face and Other Day did the only thing he could do—he bit part of Cut Nose's nose off.

That ended the fight. Cut Nose thought his entire nose was gone, but only part of one side of his nose was missing. Still, there was blood everywhere. Those who had been watching were so impressed with the quantity of it that they broke the fight up and kept the fighters apart. It took a little while for both of them to settle down. Each was dragged away by several of the onlookers. Those who went with Otherday had new respect for him. After that fight, everyone knew Cut Nose by name as soon as they saw him. It was this fight that gave him his name.

From that day on there continued to be a tense antagonism between Cut Nose and Otherday, but they never fought with each other again. Their lives seemed to head in different directions and they had little contact with each other. When the whites came into the territory, Otherday began to associate with them and tried hard to learn their ways. He spent a lot of time with them trying to learn to be a farmer and he rarely crossed paths with Cut Nose, who was a prominent warrior and hunter.

Otherday and Cut Nose were destined to play equally opposite roles when serious conflict arose between the whites and the Dakotah. Otherday helped many whites escape the massacre by guiding them to safety. He became a Scout for the white soldiers and was given a large monetary award for his services at the end of the war. He married a white woman and lived out his life as a hero. Cut Nose became the leader of the Soldier's Lodge and was a very prominent figure in the massacre, personally killing, perhaps, more white people than any other warrior.

At the end of the war he was among the thirty-eight whom were hanged.

Chapter Two

ഇ ◆ ര

Cut Nose as a Young Man
Becoming a Warrior

B Y THE TIME CUT NOSE REACHED PUBERTY, he was already adept at many of the skills and activities of a warrior-hunter and, as a result, for his age, he had a great deal of respect among his friends. Consequently, many girls admired him, and he had no trouble finding girlfriends despite his mutilated nose. No one could fail to notice the fact that part of the right side of his nose was gone, and there was nothing but a gaping hole where that part of his nose used to be. He tended to try to hide this disfigurement by cocking his head slightly to the right when meeting someone for the first time. When talking to someone, he tried his best to show his good side, but one couldn't be with him for ten seconds without noticing that he was missing a large part of his nose.

Actually, there is some disagreement regarding the extent of Cut Nose's disfigurement. Descriptions of his appearance are quite widely divergent. It is easy to understand how people might disagree regarding his appearance depending on the context in which he was observed. For example, one young white man described him as, "one of the finest specimens of manhood I have ever seen, tall, straight and with agreeable features in spite of the small piece gone from the edge of one nostril," according to Warren Wakefield of Morris, Minnesota. This description came out of the context

16

of a playful episode with the young man's family in their home some time prior to the beginning of the uprising in 1862. In another context, during the uprising of 1862, Cut Nose boasted of how he had killed the man whose body was being viewed as a group of captives passed it while traveling. In this context, one of the young male mixed-blood captives said of Cut Nose, "This fiend in human shape, this man Cut Nose, presented a most forbidden [sic], horrifying spectacle. With his bloody thumb he had besmeared his naked body, with his blackened face and long bushy hair like a Zulu's, and a half nose (one of his nostrils was missing) he was by far the ugliest looking and most repulsive specimen of humanity I had ever seen," according to Gary C. Anderson and Alan R. Woolworth in *Through Dakota Eyes: Narrative Accounts of the Minnesota Indian War of 1862*. It becomes obvious that not only is beauty in the eye of the beholder, but ugliness is also.

Still, the girls liked him. He had so many girlfriends that he never settled down with any one of them. He played the field, and play he did, taking great pleasure in sneaking off to the bushes with one girl after another. Everyone knew it, and all the girls knew it, too. Cut Nose seemed to be challenged to sneak away with every girl in the village at one time or another. There were a few holdouts, but he came close to achieving his goal.

The girls didn't seem to be bothered greatly by his "teepee creeping," which was what such promiscuity was called, but the other boys and some of the older men in the village were sometimes enraged by his promiscuous mischief. However, nobody ever said anything about it to Cut Nose. Rather, the girls might be scolded or punished if they became involved with him. Even though the girls knew that they might be severely punished if they got caught, that failed to deter them to any great extent. It merely added to the excitement of it all.

Women and girls had a social status that was lower than that of men and boys. And Cut Nose had enough respect among the men that he was almost irreproachable. Cut Nose took his pleasures where he found them and was rarely criticized. He fully enjoyed the girls who took their chances with him, and likewise, he enjoyed willing women of any age.

Women who were "in their moon," or menstruating, were expected to take residence in a special lodge outside the village. They were not permitted to enter into a spiritual arena or dance or participate in any sacred activities during that time. They may have been considered to be unholy, or perhaps even unclean. Others thought women to be too spiritually powerful during menses. Another thought is that residing in the moon lodge was a privilege given to menstruating women, enabling them to get away from their normal daily labors for a few days.

But none of that bothered or concerned Cut Nose. He spent many evenings hanging around out there, near the women's moon-lodge, knowing that during this time the women were sexually neglected by their men, and at least some of them were more interested and willing then than they were at other times.

It often happened that, one at a time, two or three of the women would come out to visit and play with Cut Nose. When one returned to the lodge giggling with satisfaction after a visit with him, another one would go out to meet him. They all knew he would be out there, not far off in the woods, eagerly waiting for them. He seemed to be insatiable. He fully enjoyed all of those who ventured out, even if they were old enough to be his grandmother.

Of all the possible pleasurable things that there were to do, however, Cut Nose loved hunting best. Hunting provided the food for the people of his village. Not only was it fun, it was rewarding because a good hunt would be followed with really good eating, a feast of game and vegetables that would make up for days of hunger or fasting. The people of the village were always very appreciative of the game he provided, and they would compliment him and treat him with great respect when he provided amply for all.

As a child, Cut Nose had watched his elders go away to hunt. He envied them and wished he could go with them. Prior to their departure, all the people of the village would gather to pray for a good and successful and safe hunt, and they offered tobacco to the Great Spirit. Then the hunters said their good-byes while they received the good-luck wishes of their wives and the others, the old men, and all the women and children of the village.

All the hunters would mount their horses, all together, and then they would mill around for just a little while, wheeling their horses about, laughing, sometimes raising a weapon in the air or swinging a tomahawk, and there would be frequent whoops and hollers. It was a joyous time. Upon a signal of the leader of the hunting party, the whole party would whoop and yell and scream in various expressions of enthusiasm as they headed off at a gallop toward the horizon, disappearing in a great cloud of dust, the noise gradually fading as they went away. Everyone watched until the hunters were out of earshot and out of sight. Their departure was always very impressive and full of optimism.

The whole village, with few exceptions, would turn out to see the hunters off. With their departure, everyone would quietly go to their own teepee to settle down. As soon as the hunters were out of sight it would be quiet, at least relatively speaking. A dog might bark, and the sound of the dog barking would stand out against the quiet. A few minutes before, while the hunters were leaving, the same dog barking would not have been heard. Many of the people remaining would go to their lodges to sleep some, likely tired from being awake much of the previous night helping to prepare the men for the hunting trip.

For Cut Nose, watching the hunters depart was very frustrating because he wanted so desperately to go with them. At his age he was not yet considered a man, and only the men were allowed to go on the hunts. To Cut Nose it seemed that childhood would last forever. He could not wait that long, and, in fact, he was able to reduce his frustration somewhat by hunting small game near the village. He would do that diligently as part of his practice for the day when he would be permitted to go on the hunts for bigger game and eventually—and more important to him—on war parties in conflicts with the Ojibwa.

In the traditional culture, an Indian was a creature of natural law and respected all life forms, including the animals that were hunted. A man had to cultivate a range of skills to be a good hunter. The most accomplished hunters were given the responsibility to provide from the village. It was an honor to be recognized as a good hunter and was a man's solemn duty to be a good provider. Next to being an accomplished warrior, being a recognized hunter was most desired.

A good hunter had to develop the ability to "think" like an animal and to cultivate the instincts of an animal. He had to be able to read nature's signs and sense things—like foul weather coming, animal behavior, and be able to read the stars for directions. He had to know how to enter the natural world unseen and unheard, to become part of it. Above all, a good hunter had to have the utmost respect for the earth and all living things or his senses would be dulled. As a youth, Cut Nose strove to acquire the necessary skills to be a good hunter.

Cut Nose liked to hunt small game by himself, alone, because he had much better luck that way. When he had others with him, they might scare the game by making noise or otherwise alerting game to their presence. Alone, Cut Nose could sneak up close to a target animal for a good killing shot. He became one of the best hunters of small game in the village. In fact he was so good that he was recognized as a major provider while the older hunters were away. He brought many birds and fish and small animals to the village when others came back empty handed. Occasionally he would kill a deer, and the village would prepare a feast.

It was on such an occasion that the main hunting party for the village returned after having had almost no success at all. Because they were nearly empty handed, the hunters had anticipated only sadness, empty bellies, and hungry villagers greeting them. And the hunters, too, were very hungry, as well as exhausted after their long hunt. Instead of sadness, however, the hunters found merriment and feasting as Cut Nose had returned to the camp after having killed not just one but two large deer the previous day. The food was plentiful and the hunters ate their fill.

The warriors laughed and joked that they should always leave Cut Nose behind to hunt for the village while they were gone because he was so good at that, but leaving Cut Nose behind in the future was only a joke. It was evident to everyone at that point that he had become a skilled hunter and was exceptionally adept at all the things a warrior needed to do. Despite his relatively young age, from then on he would be considered to be a warrior and would accompany the men of the village on all the hunting parties and war parties that left the village.

After the warriors of the village conducted a secret initiation ceremony, a special ceremonial dance was held to recognize Cut Nose as a man and a warrior. Everyone in the village attended this grand festival at which Cut Nose was the center of attention. He proudly accepted a horse that was ceremoniously presented to him as an acknowledgement of his accomplishments. Now he was entitled to all the respect and privileges that came with being a warrior.

Chapter Three

ℬ ✦ ℭ

Getting to Know White Men

As a child, Cut Nose had seen white men only rarely. Though he had been told much about them, there were no white men in his world most of the time. There were places where there were many white men, but Indians did not go there as a rule. The only white men that Cut Nose had seen were the trappers and traders who made infrequent visits to his village. So it was a very curious thing to see when the white men first started a village near the Minnesota River. They wore clothing like he had never seen before. They spoke a strange tongue. They carried with them many things that were new and never seen before, such as various kinds of guns, varieties of steel traps to catch animals, bottles made of glass, and iron pots and pans with which to cook food. All of these things were new to Cut Nose, and he wanted to discover and learn about many of these things, simple everyday things to the white man that were absolutely wondrous for this young Indian, seeing them for the first time. For a while, it seemed that the white man was harmless and even a blessing, bearing good things that could be useful. Often he would give these things to the Indians in exchange for the common goods that the Indians had, such as furs. Sometimes he even gave these wondrous things just to be friendly, asking nothing in return. How could anyone object to that?

For many years the Indians had welcomed the white man every time the white man came to visit. Now, some friendly white men were staying in a place by the river for a long time. They cut trees and used them to make a house there. Then the Indians would visit the house sometimes, and the white people would always welcome them and offer food cooked in the iron pots and pans. The Indians liked to visit the white man's house. The house itself and all of the white man's things were so new, good, useful, and interesting that the Indians wanted these things.

But over a long period of time, the whites gradually became stingy. They would keep all the good things for themselves. They told the Indians to go away and not to visit anymore. This was not a big problem to the Indians, because they had many places to go, and there were many animals to hunt and plenty of food to eat. It did bother them a little when the white people said not to visit anymore, but who knew? Maybe the Indians would not want to visit the white man again anyway. Still, when they said, in effect, "Go away," it felt like rejection. It was not friendly.

Later, when the Indians did visit again, there were two houses by the river, and there were more white men, and two white women. The Indians thought it was good that there were more of them, because now the white people would not be lonely. The Indians offered them some meat, thinking that now there were many mouths to feed, and they might be hungry. The whites took the meat, but they offered nothing in return, not even a meal or some soup. The Indians camped nearby, but the whites did not invite them into their houses. Also, the whites did not visit the Indians. After two days, the Indians went to another place thinking that the whites were not very polite or friendly.

Almost any element of the white culture had an exact opposite in the Indian culture. Indians viewed whites as materialistic, individualistic and self-centered, and the Indians thought it odd that whites embraced nuclear families. The Dakotah kept personal possessions to a minimum, which fit well with their nomadic lifestyle. Everything one owned would have to be moved; it made sense to them to keep only those things they needed. A person who hoarded possessions was thought to be greedy and selfish.

Europeans typically arrived with large wagons filled with possessions, most of which the Indians did not own.

The settlers sought comfort and an easy life style. Their women were protected somewhat from hardships and harshness. The Dakotah maintained only minimum comforts, and Dakotah women expected and accepted a hard life. White traders bargained for merchandise and tried to get the best of every deal. The Dakotah traded with a sharing mentality and were, therefore, vulnerable to being cheated. Whites believed Indians were subhuman. For the Dakotah, the ultimate goal in life was to explore their humanity, and it was quite ironic that, ultimately, Indians saw whites as barbarians without human conscience.

The whites had camped and built their houses near a place the Indians often went to cross the river. This place came to be known as "Traverse de Sioux." The water was shallow there and the crossing was easy, especially in late summer when the level of the river was low. Many Indians liked to camp for several days at this place because they would meet others and exchange news and make new acquaintances. It was somewhat annoying that the whites had taken some of the best camping sites for their houses and tents, but there was an abundance of room, so the Indians merely chose alternative sites without complaint. Later, when more whites came and even some of the good alternative sites were taken, there was more annoyance.

For Cut Nose, rejection by the white men was very frustrating. He liked white men, and he was fascinated by the many good things that the white men had. He liked the food the white men ate. And sometimes he was given a drink of whiskey and he liked that—it made him feel good. So he sought out ways to spend time with white men. He tried to learn their language, so he could understand more about them, and it wasn't long before he could have a fairly good conversation with them, but always in their language. There were very few white men who could speak Dakotah or who wanted to learn how to do so.

The ability to communicate with the whites actually served Cut Nose well in many instances. His communication skills landed him a job with Joseph N. Nicollet, the French explorer. Nicollet launched an expedition to look over the area of what is now southern Minnesota in September of 1838. He hired several Indian guides to accompany him on this expedition, and one of them was Cut Nose,[4] referred to by Nicollet as "Nez Coupee." Cut Nose had eagerly jumped at the opportunity to be a guide for Nicollet when he learned that Nicollet was looking for a few Indian guides. Although Cut Nose was slightly less than twenty years of age, Nicollet hired him right away because he was well recommended by the others and could speak English fairly well. However, Nicollet fired Cut Nose after only ten days, reporting that he had failed to be a man of his word.

The way he failed to keep his word is not described in Nicollet's notes, but one might guess that it had to do with Cut Nose's drinking. Nicollet would not have put up with much of that. The records indicate that Cut Nose was later paid the sum of ten dollars for his services to Nicollet, although Nicollet had authorized "goods of his own selection to the amount of $10." It is possible that Nicollet didn't want Cut Nose paid in cash, knowing that the young man would likely just blow it on whiskey. Joseph Nicollet may have been the first to recognize that Cut Nose had a problem with alcohol.

The Dakotahs had never possessed a social stimulant such as alcohol and didn't have a need for it in their culture. With the use of alcohol, the Indians discovered a strange sensation that made them feel better about themselves. Alcohol intoxication was a shortcut to the same feeling of elation that came with being honored for some great accomplishment. Being the great deceiver that it is, alcohol made the Indians falsely proud, made them like themselves, and made them expect others to like them too. It relieved them of inhibitions that controlled their behavior, and it caused them to do things they would not otherwise do. It made them feel brave, and bravery was the most highly valued trait in their culture. Cut Nose was an ambitious young man and quickly became a victim of alcohol.

One day, while visiting at the new village called Traverse de Sioux with some of his companions, Cut Nose was admiring the large riverboat that was moored at the nearby landing. He had not seen such a large boat up close before. It had a large paddle wheel in the back and that, too, was something Cut Nose had never seen before up close. From the shore of the river, he had seen this big steamboat going up and down the river many times, however, and had shouted greetings to the man riding on it, but the man had never responded with anything more than a stare. Cut Nose had never had a previous opportunity to look at the boat up close while it was moored.

Dr. W.W. Mayo, the owner and operator of this boat, was busy taking some cargo off his boat and putting other cargo on board. He was aware of the four Indians watching him, but he paid no attention to them. Cut Nose recognized him as the man who had been on the boat the many times he had seen the boat on the water.

"Who is that man?" he asked a white man he knew from the village of Traverse de Sioux.

"That's Doctor Mayo on his boat," was the reply.

"What does he do?"

"He's a doctor, and he also runs this boat."

Many English words were still unknown to Cut Nose, and he had never heard the word "doctor" before. "What is a Doctor?" he asked.

"He helps people who are sick."

"He prays for them?"

"Maybe sometimes, but he mainly gives them medicine."

"We have a doctor in my village, too," said Cut Nose. "He rides the boat everywhere?"

"Oh, no. He goes with the boat one time in seven days to Jordan, then to Mankato, then back to LeSueur. He has a horse that he rides most of the time when he is doin' his doctoring."

"Why?"

"Why what?"

"Why does he go with boat?"

"People pay him money to carry things on his boat."

"Good. I understand. Easy to carry many things on big boat, get much money."

"Yes, I think he does make a lot of money."

Cut Nose continued to watch as Dr. Mayo worked to put on board all the things piled at the landing. Cut Nose noted with special interest that some of the cargo appeared to be whiskey. Dr. Mayo worked hard. He was a small man and struggled greatly with some of the larger boxes. In fact, Dr. Mayo's size was so diminutive that he was widely known as "the little doctor." Cut Nose wanted to go on the boat and offer to help the little man with a particularly large box, thinking he might be rewarded with a drink of whiskey.

But Dr. Mayo said, "No, I can handle it. Just stay out of the way." He probably had certain ways of doing things and just preferred to do them himself rather than trying to get someone else to do things his way.

Cut Nose thought Dr. Mayo was not a very friendly man, and he gave up on the thought that he might get a drink, but he continued to watch until the boat was all loaded. Then Dr. Mayo started the steam engine, stoked the fire up a bit, and started the paddle wheel to pull the boat off the shore and away from the landing. When the boat was at midstream, the paddle wheel stopped and then started again, this time pushing the boat upstream. Cut Nose watched with rapt fascination until the boat was well upstream and disappeared around a bend in the river. Even then he could still hear the chugging of the steam engine, and he found some satisfaction in just listening.

Steam boating on the Minnesota River was a risky business for many reasons. Almost every spring, the river would be flooded and turbulent, and at such times the big boat was hard to control. Every autumn the river became so shallow that in many places it was barely navigable. And, of course, in the winter it was frozen closed. But during the summer season the little doctor could augment his meager income from his medical practice with good cash income from the freight business. When he could not use his boat, he continued to haul freight with a horse and wagon.

When Cut Nose first met white men, they were friendly. Almost right away they introduced him to whiskey. There are people who react to whiskey like it is poison the first time they taste it, but Cut Nose liked it right from the start, and from the very beginning he couldn't get enough of it. He would keep drinking as long as there was any whiskey left to drink or until he passed out, whichever came first. If he passed out, he would start trying to find more whiskey as soon as he woke up. He was a natural born drinker and seemed to love being as drunk as he could get. Getting drunk turned into his main ambition.

The Indians didn't know how to make whiskey, and the only source they had for it was the white man. So Cut Nose would hang around the white man's settlement at Traverse de Sioux and try to trade for whiskey. He would give to the white man just about anything that was asked for whiskey. He would do any kind of work, run errands, fish, hunt, collect hides, even trade his own clothing for a bottle of whiskey. As soon as he got his hands on a bottle it was gone and he would be after another. This went on for a couple of years.

At first, Cut Nose was sure he was having a good time when he was drinking. At least, while drinking, things happened that seemed at the time to be memorably joyful—even if he couldn't remember them later.

On one such occasion, he had an encounter with the little doctor from LeSueur, W.W. Mayo, which was certainly memorable for Doctor Mayo, whether or not Cut Nose could later recall it. It was on a beautiful day, partly cloudy, with mild temperatures and no wind at all. The birds were singing in the trees, and the morning sun was sparkling on the nearby river. Cut Nose and two friends were still reeling from an entire night of hard drinking. They had traded some beaded buckskin boots for a gallon jug of whiskey the evening before, and they had spent the entire night drinking it while sitting around the campfire and telling stories. They had camped just upstream from Traverse de Sioux right on the edge of the woods next to the river.

His friends were tired and slowing down a lot and ready for a nap in the sun, but Cut Nose wasn't quite done yet—which was not uncommon. As a rule, if there was anything left to drink, Cut Nose was not quite done. With the whiskey jug in his hand, he headed into the woods to get more firewood. It was his intention to perk up the fire to cook some fish that he had yet to catch. Catching them would not be much of a problem, even as drunk as he was. There were plenty of fish in the river.

He had picked up only a couple of sticks when he heard something approaching on the trail through the woods. This trail was not heavily traveled and could be described as the scenic route along the river. The other trail, the one that most people usually followed, was on the other side of the woods that bordered the river, perhaps a quarter mile from the river's shore, along the edge of the woods. That trail was always dry, while this one was flooded sometimes if the river ran high.

Cut Nose watched as a man on horseback emerged from the woods up the trail. As the rider came closer, he recognized him to be Doctor Mayo, the man who rode the boat. "Hey, Mayo," he said as the rider approached, "you don't ride the boat today."

Mayo brought his horse to a halt. "Whoa," he said, as Cut Nose now approached, "No, not today. What do you want?"

Mayo's question reflected some surprise and some uneasiness over encountering anyone on this out-of-the-way trail. He had taken this trail because it was a nice day and offered many beautiful, picturesque views of the river. It was a very pleasant ride along the river, but he had not expected to find anyone there.

Cut Nose took Doctor Mayo's question literally. "I want your horse," he said. He didn't mean that he was going to take it. "You have a very nice horse," he said in a complimentary way. He was only trying to have a friendly conversation, and the question. "What do you want?" seemed to require some such response, at least from Cut Nose's perspective. And after all, Doctor Mayo was rich. That he might actually want to give something to Cut Nose was the wishful and hopeful and quite intoxicated thought that Cut Nose had had all at once. "And you have a big boat, too," Cut Nose added.

"Well, the horse is not for sale," replied the doctor, who knew full well that Cut Nose was not offering to buy it. The horse was nervous, perhaps sensing the rider's nervousness, and Cut Nose took hold of the bridle to steady the horse while finishing the conversation.

"You can give the horse to me," Cut Nose said.

"Are you crazy?"

"No, look," said Cut Nose, holding the horse's bridle with one hand and extending the whiskey jug toward the doctor with the other, offering the doctor a drink.

"You've been drinking. You're drunk!" observed Doctor Mayo, showing obvious disapproval with this tone of voice.

"Drunk? What is drunk?"

"You've had too much to drink."

"Oh, no, we drink whiskey—not too much—we like it. Here, have some," again offering the jug.

By now Mayo had stood for all that he could tolerate. "Get away," he ordered as he slapped at Cut Nose with his riding crop. Flinching away from the crop, Cut Nose let go of the horse's bridle and backed off as Doctor Mayo spurred his horse and rode off.

Cut Nose watched the little doctor ride away and disappear down the trail through the woods. He was quite perplexed by this whole interaction, but he was too drunk to care much more about it. He came to the conclusion that he had been right all along in thinking that Doctor Mayo is simply not a very friendly man.

Eventually, Cut Nose became quite well known for his drinking. He was drunk most of the time. He lost a lot of respect among white people as a result of the extent to which he would lower himself and grovel to get a drink. It was not so much a question of what he would do to get a drink as what he wouldn't do—and the answer was that he'd do just about anything. He was hooked. He was the worst drunk around.

The whites began to take advantage of him while he was so desperate for whiskey. Whenever something disagreeable had to be done, they looked for Cut Nose to do it in exchange for drink. They would offer less reward for doing a job than it was worth because they knew that he would take the job anyway. He thought that he was being friendly to help out the way he did, and he thought the white man was being friendly by paying him with whiskey.

It took him over two years to realize how he was being humiliated. Many of his friends had told him that his drinking was disgracing him, but for a long time he couldn't understand that or accept it. He was not available to participate in hunting parties because he was too busy having parties of his own. He would get others to join him in his drinking, and some of the other young men of the tribe became just as irresponsible as Cut Nose.

When Cut Nose was drunk, which was most of the time, he liked to fight. That is, after all, what he did best. He was fierce and sometimes picked fights for no reason at all. He would not fight white men, but he would jump all over his closest friends, the ones who were his drinking buddies.

He was not available for the protection of the village. He was not spending much time hunting to provide for the village, and, when he did hunt, he often traded the game to the white men for whiskey. When his feelings of guilt grew to be a large burden, he sometimes blamed those around him for it. After all, they, too, were neglecting their responsibilities even if it was Cut Nose, himself, who had instigated their lack of responsibility.

Cut Nose came to be severely criticized by the more responsible members of the tribe. He was about to be stripped of all the leadership positions that he had been given.

When at last it finally became clear to Cut Nose that all of his critics were right, he quit drinking completely. To his everlasting credit, he wouldn't touch a drop. He went away, by himself, unaccompanied, on a hunting trip. He traveled to places where there were no white men and no whiskey. Although he was not a particularly religious man, he prayed for spiritual guidance. He was gone for most of a summer.

When he returned, he had sobered up, and he was a different person. He had a great deal of anger for the whites, recalling how he had been used by them. White men would approach him to do things for them as they had before, degrading things that most men would not willingly do without great compensation, and they would offer only a small bottle of whiskey. To their surprise, Cut Nose would decline the job and decline the whiskey. He even avoided speaking to them in English if he could get by with it. He wanted to speak only Dakotah. To himself, he would make a mental note of the offer, and, with his sober judgment, he would also make a special note of the extent to which this "friend" was being friendly. He thought to himself that some time in the future he would make such friends sorry for offering that kind of "friendship." As it turned out, this time was not far off. Cut Nose would get his chance to vent his anger at the whites sooner and more completely than he could imagine.

While he had been away that summer, much had happened. His people were hungry. They were tired of eating the white man's rice, and now the white man was refusing to give even that. The agreements which had been established with the whites and the white man's promises were worth nothing. Promises did not relieve hunger. The people were suffering. Game was scarce. The whites would not listen to the complaints of the Indians.

Chapter Four

ഉ ✦ ൙

The Broken Treaties: Unexpected Results and Promises Unfulfilled

T HE DAKOTAH NATION MADE SEVERAL TREATIES with the white people. In various treaties, the Indians gave large amounts of land to the white people in exchange for goods and money, which were supposed to put the Indians on easy street forever. In 1805 the Dakotah gave up all of the area of what is now Minneapolis and St Paul for some presents, some whiskey, and $2,000 from the United States government. In 1837 they ceded all of their land east of the Mississippi River. They thought that they were not giving up very much because they didn't live there anymore anyway.

The Minnesota River Valley contains a significant part of the history of the State of Minnesota. Prior to the treaty of 1851, when the treaty of Traverse des Sioux was entered into, the entire bottom one-third of the present day state of Minnesota and parts of Wisconsin, Iowa, and South Dakota were the homelands of the Dakotah Sioux. The Dakotah Sioux is the Eastern Division of the Sioux Nation. The other two divisions are the Yankton and Yanktonai, who make up the Middle Sioux Division (called the Nakotah), and the Lakotah, who are the Western Division.

When one thinks of Sioux Indians, the first picture that comes to mind is that of the plains Indians who hunted the buffalo. The Western or Lakotah

33

Sioux fit that image. The Dakotah Sioux, however, were originally a woodland people with a woodland culture. The Dakotah consisted of four bands: the Sisseton and Wahpeton bands (later known as the Upper Sioux) and the Mdewakanton and Wahpekute bands (later known as the Lower Sioux). The Upper Sioux Agency was near present day Granite Falls, Minnesota, and the Lower Sioux Agency was near present day Morton, Minnesota.

In 1849 Minnesota became an official territory of the United States and settlers began to move in by the tens of thousands. Nearly all of the rest of the land in Minnesota was, in effect, just taken from the Dakotah by the United States when Minnesota officially was designated a territory. What had been Dakotah hunting grounds became farms. Fences were built to mark them off. Cows grazed where buffaloes once roamed. Increasingly, the Dakotah people were irritated when they went to a favorite hunting place and found, instead of game, only a newly built log cabin, chickens pecking in the yard, and cows in fenced-in fields. Everywhere, game was getting more and more scarce, killed or forced away by the white people who were flooding the whole territory. It is clear now, in retrospect, that when the Dakotah signed the treaties relinquishing their land to the whites, they did not fully understand that they were opening the floodgates for such a huge deluge of white farmers. And they certainly didn't understand that the whites would own the land to the exclusion of the Indians. They had little understanding of the entire concept of land ownership.

What started out as easy land concessions for the Dakotah to make became more difficult as more and more whites poured into the territory. At first, the Dakotah thought there was plenty of land and enough room for everyone. After a while they were not so sure because there were so many whites, and the whites were so hungry for the land and gobbled up so much of it. The Dakotah found themselves hungry for food, and they became increasingly hungry as their hunting grounds were destroyed. Eventually, they didn't give in so easily to the tactics of the whites to persuade them to sign treaties yielding even more ground.

The tactics of the white treaty negotiators included everything from sugar-coated sweet talk and presents to glowing promises of lives of leisure for the Dakotah people, who would have bellies eternally full of wonderful food. Another tactic was to threaten that if the Dakotah refused to cooperate they would be forced by large armies of soldiers to leave the area anyway.

To back up these threats, and for other reasons as well, arrangements were made for many Indian chiefs to visit Washington, D.C., to talk with the "White Fathers," who were the people with authority in the government of the United States. Many chiefs did make this trip and were able to see for themselves the large populations of whites in the eastern part of the United States. They could conclude for themselves, and many did so, that it would be utterly futile to resist the onslaught of the whites.

Large amounts of rice were provided to the Indians as food commodities, part of the payments to the Indians for Indian lands ceded to the whites through the agreements established in the Treaties of 1851 and 1857. There are many kinds of rice. This was a white rice, imported from distant places, possibly even from China. The Dakotah knew nothing about this kind of rice. They knew a lot about various kinds of grain that they harvested locally, and they knew about the wild rice that grew up north along the lakeshores, harvested mostly by the Ojibwa. Wild rice was often part of the booty taken from Ojibwa warriors after a battle with them. It was a very flavorful grain used in stews and soups and, less often, eaten as a side dish by itself. It was not at all like the white rice that was being provided as a commodity by the government.

The Dakotah didn't care much for the white rice, but they had bags and bags of it. They were told to boil it and use it as a staple. But boiled, it looked like a lot of maggots to the Dakotah. It was quite unappetizing in its appearance, and by itself didn't have much flavor. Still, it filled the belly and was better than starvation. So, they ate it.

Nevertheless, much of the rice was wasted. Spilled on the ground, it was scattered and lost in the grass. If it got wet, it rotted quickly. Commodities were sometimes spoiled even before the Indians received them. If the rice was rotten, many real maggots developed, and the maggots were so much like the rice in their appearance that they were difficult to see. The Dakotah developed the general rule that the rice should be eaten only if it didn't move. A lot of it was not edible. Still, if they were hungry enough, they would eat the rice even if it did have maggots in it. They could get most of the maggots and other worms out of it by boiling the rice in water—the worms would float and could be easily picked out. They would fry the rice after it was cooked. Frying it in some fat after it was boiled would give the rice a more palatable flavor.

Another commodity provided by the government was beans. Sometimes the rice was mixed with the beans in preparation for eating. Usually there would be some game meat to throw in the pot also. With a little ingenuity, some very tasty dishes were prepared, and life was not all that bad, most of the time. At least their bellies could be full. However, a full belly was not always completely satisfying. Living this way, depending on the government for survival, was certainly not a good life.

Sometimes the Indians had full bellies when the local settlers were having a lot of hunger. This would happen if the weather destroyed local crops. Crops would fail sometimes if it rained too little and the crops dried up. Crops failed also if it rained too much and the fields were flooded. Even in good times life was hard for the settlers. But in bad times the settlers' life was extra hard. If they could not provide for themselves, it was certain that they had no money with which to purchase provisions. The government didn't provide for them. When they saw how the government did provide for the Indians while the settlers were suffering so much themselves, they were understandably angry. It was hard for them to understand why the Indians complained. All in all, there was more than enough frustration to go around for everyone.

Eventually, the Dakotah became disgusted with the way things were developing since the white man came into their lives. Not only was life simply stagnating and not very satisfying, but eventually the lives of many of the people were actually being threatened with starvation. It is said that whenever a nation is in trouble, listening to the daily conversations of the people can identify the real nature of the problems. This was certainly true of the Dakotah people in Minnesota at the time.

Many people among the Dakotah were talking about how life had changed for the worse since the white man arrived, and how hard times had come upon them. A war with the whites to take back the land or eject the white violators of the land who wasted the game, was discussed more and more, becoming closer to being a possibility. There was a lot of tension on both sides.

The war of 1862 was really over ruined hunting grounds, farms cropping up in places where for many lifetimes there had been good hunting. The white man was taking the land that belonged to the Indian. There had been buffaloes on this land before the white man came, but now the buffaloes were gone. There were still many buffaloes on the prairies of the West where there were not yet many white men. Eventually, white men would cause the near extinction of all the buffaloes.[5]

The most heated talk of war took place in the Soldier's Lodge among the "blanket Indians." These Indians were conservatives, traditionalists, as opposed to the "Pantaloons," or farmer Indians, who were converting to the ways of the whites. Half-breeds and farmer Indians were not allowed to enter the Soldier's Lodge. The members of the Soldier's Lodge were all full bloods, braves, hunters, and warriors. Some of the tribal chiefs attended meetings of the Soldier's Lodge, but others didn't. Sometimes tribal decisions were influenced more by the leaders of the Soldier's Lodge than by the various chiefs in the tribe. Cut Nose was certainly one of the more prominent leaders, if not the most prominent, in the Soldier's Lodge at that time.

There had been treaties, but the white man did not honor them. The whites did not keep up their end of the bargains that had been struck. When the treaties were made with the whites, the Dakotah had little idea of what these treaties would lead to in terms of the white man taking over. The encroachment of the whites on the land was different from what the Ojibwa had tried to do when they sought to move into Dakotah territories. The Ojibwa had not tried to own the land or fence it in, and yet even their encroachments were enough to stimulate the Dakotah to take them on in mortal combat. When white men presumed to own the land to the exclusion of the Dakotah, the anger that resulted was enormous.

In direct violation of the conditions of the treaty of 1857, there were German settlers encroaching on land that was part of the Indian reservation. The Indians complained to the government about this. The government had the responsibility to protect the rights of the Indians, but instead of moving the whites out of the reservation, the government redrew the boundary lines and let the white settlers stay. The Indians realized that the government had little concern for their rights or the contracts they had made in the treaties. The white settlers knew they were on disputed land, yet they stubbornly stayed. In many ways, the government and the white settlers themselves contributed to the start of the war.

To add even more to the anger of the Dakotah people, other promises the whites made were not being kept. Payment of the money that was promised in the treaties was due in June of 1862, and in August was still unpaid. The Indians knew that if and when the money would be paid, the traders would get the money they were owed by the Indians first, and there might be little left over for the Indians themselves. The traders had extended credit to the Indians when the payments were delayed. While this was a needed and considerate practice on the part of the traders, problems developed because of the manner in which some traders initiated their reimbursements from the government. The Indians believed some of the amounts owed were wrong, and some even claimed they owned nothing since they were producing food from gardens and small farms. The Indians kept no records and had to rely exclusively on the word of the traders with whom they dealt. The government ignored their complaints and continued to make direct payments to the traders.

The people on the reservations were broke and hungry—in fact, they were starving. Their crops had failed because of drought. What wasn't dried up was finished off by swarms of grasshoppers. There was nothing left to eat. It seemed more and more evident to the Indians that the white man was deliberately trying to exterminate the Dakotah, and, in fact, was treating the Dakotah people like unwanted animals, pests that they wished to be rid of completely.

There were many events that occurred that were persuasive support for that belief. One such incident occurred when a group of Indian leaders went to the food storage warehouse at the Upper Sioux Reservation to plead for the distribution of food, as many of their people were hungry. The traders and government representatives with whom they talked had little appreciation for how desperate the Indians actually were and denied their request for food even though the food was available in abundance. The Indians knew that there was plenty of food in the warehouses and were not satisfied by the bureaucratic reasons given for the refusals to distribute it. They didn't understand such bureaucratic reasoning. Furthermore, one of the traders exacerbated the anger and frustration of the Indians by saying, "If they're hungry, let 'em eat grass." He was speaking through an interpreter and might have assumed that the comment would not have been repeated or translated, but some of the Indians present understood him perfectly without a translation. This comment clearly suggested that the whites considered the Indians to be animals. With that statement, the conversation was over, and the Indians departed not only frustrated, but also insulted and extremely angry.

Some of the people did not believe, at first, that the whites actually wanted to exterminate or kill them all, and they took some convincing. The skeptics argued that they had been treated nicely and in a friendly manner by some whites. But there were plenty of stories about how friendly whites had turned unfriendly. Cut Nose repeatedly recalled how he was treated during his drinking days and felt that he had many scores to settle.

Over a period of many years, some Indians had practically become white men, they were so much assimilated. They dressed like whites, acted like whites, became Christians, went to the white man's church, sent their children to attend white schools, lived in houses like whites, spoke English, could read and write English, and they made a living by farming the land. Some even married white women. John Otherday, the same man who bit off part of Cut Nose's nose, was a prominent example of this kind of Indian. There were many Indian-white marriages. It would not be easy to separate the Indians from the whites again.

The whites gave such Indians favored status. If commodities were available to the Indians through the treaty agreements, these assimilated Indians got them for sure. The blanket Indians were equally entitled to such handouts, but they got them only when there was plenty to go around. Like many of the local settlers, blanket Indians often went hungry even when farmer Indians had plenty.[6]

It should be noted that there were also some whites who, for all intents and purposes, became Indians. Of the thirty-eight warriors hanged in Mankato after the Uprising, three were half-breeds. One of the thirty-eight, ironically, was a completely white boy, only sixteen years old, though his white captors thought he was an Indian. The Indians knew he was white, but they didn't let on. He appeared in every way to be an Indian. His complexion was dark, and his hair was black and straight. He dressed in buckskins and spoke only the Dakotah language. It is likely that he believed himself to be an Indian, as well, but he was white without a drop of Indian blood. He had been born to a white couple at a lumber camp and both parents died while he was still an infant. The orphan was given to an Indian woman who cared for him and raised him as her own child among the Indians.

The Dakotah were aware that many white men had left the area to fight in a war with other white men in the South. The year was 1862, and the Civil War was well under way at this time. Many young men had departed the area to serve in the Union Army. The Indians had noticed their absence and, in some cases, had even talked with some of the young men as they were preparing to leave, learning that these men were expecting to be gone in the service of the army for a very long time.

There was discussion about the "Renville Rangers," a troop of local men comprised of recently recruited volunteers, mostly half-breed Indians, who had just left the area to go to fight in the Civil War. Many of the Indians thought that the whites must be pretty hard up to resort to recruiting half-breeds. The Indians believed that the Renville Rangers, about forty in number, had left the area to go to fight the Confederacy hundreds of miles away in the South. In fact, they had traveled only as far as St Peter by the time the uprising developed, so they were diverted from the Civil War to be used as reinforcements for the Army at nearby Fort Ridgely. There the half-breeds actually faced the Dakotah in battle despite the fact that many of the Dakotah warriors were their own close relatives.

The Indians observed that with many young white men gone away to fight in another war, the white settlers that remained in the area were relatively vulnerable and unprotected. In these circumstances, it might be easy to drive all the whites out of the whole territory. The whites were trespassing according to established agreements, and this was Indian land in the first place. The Indians had tried in every way possible to reason with the whites, but the whites appeared to be unresponsive to reason. Driving the whites out, ordering them to go away, and then if they would not leave, forcing them to go away—this seemed to be the only solution. And if none of these measures worked, the whites could be killed.

It sounded so simple, but on further consideration it became evident that there was much more to it. What if the whites resisted when they were being forced? When thinking about it at first, most of the people couldn't believe that with so many of the young white men gone the whites remaining would be so stupid as to try to resist the whole Dakotah Nation. But then again, it was well known and obvious that the whites were not very reasonable.

It was decided that, should they resist, they would have to be killed. So the main "program" of the proposed war became one of reclaiming the Indian land by forcing the whites to leave, and killing the whites who refused to go. The end result should be no whites in the land of the Dakotah nation, and in the future, the Dakotah would never make another treaty to sell their land. That was the plan.

Genocide was something that the Indians had never before considered, and the very idea of it was hard to crystallize in their minds. It was a thought so evil, so vicious, and so foreign, that it was hard for them to conceive of it at all. It was shocking to them, but, as the concept continued to grow in their thinking, they become convinced that the white men were systematically trying to eliminate them. Therefore, they reasoned, they had no choice but to fight if they were to survive at all. And in retaliation for the genocidal treatment given to them by the whites, they developed a program of their own that was something like genocide, a plan to get rid of all the whites.

Despite their belief that the whites were intending to wipe the Dakotah out, kill them all, exterminate them, practice genocide, the Indians rationalized that they would not respond in kind, exactly. They would not be guilty of such a despicable thing. They merely wanted the return of what was rightfully theirs, their land. If the whites would merely leave the area and not come back, that would be fine. They could go elsewhere and live any way they would choose, but not here, not in Dakotah Territory. They had behaved in some ways that were quite unacceptable. They were no longer welcomed, and they must leave or die.

The land was the home of the Dakotah in which the whites had been guests. The whites had been welcomed in the beginning, but they had behaved badly, stayed too long, ate too much, and now were being asked to leave. If they refused to leave they would be told to leave. If then they still refused to leave, they would be kicked out. Then, if they wouldn't go, they would be killed. If they did choose to go, they would be killed if they came back. If they would only leave and not come back, then everyone could live happily ever after. What an unrealistic dream this turned out to be after all was said and done! But in the miserable circumstances that existed at the time, many believed it.

Chapter Five

ɞ ◆ ʚ

Slaughter of White Settlers

T HE 1862 SIOUX INDIAN UPRISING actually began when four Indian men murdered five people at a place far north and east of the Lower Sioux Reservation. It happened on a Sunday, the seventeenth of August, 1862. The Indians had been on a hunting trip and were on their way home, frustrated and empty handed. They'd had some luck finding whiskey, but no luck at all finding game. They were going to be embarrassed about that when they got home because they knew that the hungry people at home were counting on them for food. They were hungry also, and tired, and very annoyed and angry over how many of their favorite hunting places were now occupied by white farmers, who seemed to be everywhere.

The killing followed an argument among the Indians themselves, when they found a few chicken eggs near a white man's homestead. Because they were so hungry, these eggs were like a gift from God, but one of the four said that it wasn't right to take them, that the eggs belonged to the whites and taking them would cause trouble. This triggered the one with the eggs to throw them to the ground, breaking them, and to call the other a coward. To prove that he was not a coward, that young hunter said that he would kill the whites in the homestead, and if his companions were not cowards, they would join him. At that point the war began.

The Indians approached the whites in a friendly manner to put them off guard. They asked for some whiskey but were refused. They ended up killing five of the eight people present at the homestead. When the shooting started, two women and a boy were able to hide. They survived, probably because the Indians didn't even know they were there. The four Indians then took horses and headed for home as fast as they could travel, arriving at the Lower Sioux Reservation late that night.

At the reservation, the story about what had happened aroused a great deal of excitement. Everyone anticipated that there would be serious consequences that would result from the killings. Arguments ranged from turning the four guilty Indians over to the whites, at one extreme, to getting organized for an all-out assault on the whites at the other extreme. Cut Nose was totally in favor of an all-out aggressive attack on the whites.

Going to war with the whites was the option that finally won out over the better judgment of some of the local tribal leaders. The chief of the tribe, Little Crow, was opposed to the war and argued against it, expressing the opinion that this war could not be won. He warned that for each white man killed, ten would come to take his place. Still, with great reluctance, and after being called a coward for his opposition, he eventually supported the decision to fight. This decision was partly influenced by some recent political infighting that had been taking place among the Indians themselves, but it was also the culmination of the many frictions that had developed between the whites and the Indians over a long period of time. Without a doubt, hunger and desperation over frustrating circumstances contributed to it.

The values of the early Dakotahs were bravery, knowledge, fortitude, and wisdom. All of these had to do with their hunting and gathering life style. Bravery was the highest value and one that was measured in each individual Indian. Calling an Indian a coward was the greatest insult one could make. Most people today might shrug off such an insult and not be overly offended. But Little Crow overrode his own better judgment and went to war after being called a coward. In the old culture, a man became a leader (or "elder") because he could make wise decisions. Through bravery, and violence if necessary, younger men wanted to shortcut the long process of becoming an elder. The strong desire of Cut Nose to be a leader also contributed to the start of the war. He was anxious to lead the Soldier's Lodge in battle.

The debating over what to do lasted most of the night. Near daybreak, the activity turned to making preparations for the assault on the whites, gathering weapons and supplies for the fighting ahead of them. At dawn, they attacked the small white settlement at the Lower Sioux Agency. Here was a warehouse full of food, and the stores and goods of the traders, all of which would provide immediate relief of hunger in addition to materials and supplies for the continuing conflict ahead of them.

In addition to the warehouse, there were other buildings that were quarters for the Indian agent and all the others who lived and worked in this settlement. All were attacked simultaneously.

This attack was over quickly. The people living there had no warning of impending danger and were killed before they could defend themselves. Only one white man survived the attack, and he was taken prisoner. One of the first to be killed was Andrew Myrick, the trader who had said, "Let them eat grass." Long after this first attack, his body was found a hundred yards from his store at the Lower Sioux Agency, his mouth stuffed full of grass.

What happened next was the rest of the tragic 1862 Uprising. It was tragic because many people suffered horrible deaths in the conflict and nothing good came out of it. Little Crow was right—there were many more whites than anyone had imagined, and they just kept coming. Not only that, but the whites were more organized, had better weapons, and knew more about good tactics for fighting a war.

The Indians did well, at first. They scattered in little war parties and covered the countryside, killing small groups of settlers in their widespread homesteads. Very much like what had happened at the Indian agency on the reservation, an Indian war party would descend upon a homestead and kill all who were present before they even had a chance to defend themselves. The poor settlers didn't even know that there was a problem with the Indians until it was much too late. Almost all of the white people who had homesteads within thirty miles of the reservation, an estimated 500 men, women, and children, were killed in the carnage of the first two days or soon after.

The whites among the Dakotah at the time of the uprising present-ed some difficulty to many of the warriors trying to carry out the "program" of the war. It would not be easy to kill the whites with whom they had estab-lished close, personal, friendly relationships. This difficulty was not com-pletely thought out before the uprising began, and it generated a lot of con-fusion and conflict after the fighting started. For example, on the very first morning, there was a lot of disagreement about whether half-breeds should be killed. Some were killed immediately, but some were taken prisoner and held captive, and the question of whether they were to be killed was to be settled at a later date. Some half-breeds were killed even during their cap-tivity, and the threat of being killed hovered over these people constantly for three months until the uprising was over and they were ultimately released.

Even some full-blooded Indians were in danger of being killed. Many of the "farmer" Indians were well assimilated among the whites and were more like whites than Indians. Some of the blanket Indians wanted to kill them too. In fact, it was common at the start of the war for farmer Indians to quickly become blanket Indians to avoid being killed. Many of them reluc-tantly took an active part in the uprising after it started. Even in these threatening circumstances, however, some of the farmer Indians maintained their allegiances with the whites.

John Otherday was one who gave outstanding service to the white people at the time. He and Cut Nose had gone in opposite directions with their lives since even before Otherday bit off part of Cut Nose's nose. When the war broke out, Otherday led a party of sixty-two whites across the prairies from near the Lower Agency to the safety of the white settlements in the east, successfully avoiding being intercepted by any Indian war parties. If he had been caught by other Indians while doing this, he surely would have been killed. Instead of participating in the uprising with the Indians, he actu-ally was on the side of the whites, not only helping them avoid being massa-cred, but also subsequently serving the white army soldiers as a scout. It is ironic that Cut Nose and Otherday led such extremely opposite lives with respect to their involvement with the white people. Just as Cut Nose was a leader of the Indians in the war against the whites, Otherday was quite prominent among the whites in their conflict with the Indians. After the end of the war, Cut Nose was hanged. Otherday was given an award of $2,500 for the services he provided to the whites during the war. This was enough money to buy a farm and essentially live happily ever after.

However, for nearly all the people involved, this so-called Indian war or uprising was a disaster from the start. It was certainly a disaster for the many settlers scattered across the prairie. Hundreds were killed even before they knew that there was an uprising. Although the Indians suffered relatively few casualties during the actual fighting, the uprising was as much a disaster for them because they lost the war and lost everything else in the end. The fighting was over in a few short weeks. Four months after the uprising began thirty-eight warriors were hanged, and nearly all the other Dakotah Indians in the vicinity—men, women, and children alike—were captured and confined, later to be shipped (literally, like animals) out of the area, to be relocated in Nebraska.

The first settler that Cut Nose killed was a woman. He wanted only for the woman to die quickly, without suffering. He told her to get on her knees and pray. She did pray on her knees with her head lowered slightly and her eyes closed as Cut Nose moved behind her and struck her on the head with his war club. In his determination to kill her instantly and mercifully, he struck a mighty blow—much too mighty as it turned out. The business end of the weapon punched through the woman's cranium without slowing until the handle of the weapon stopped it. Bloody brains flew in every direction, Cut Nose being splashed with some of them in the process. To add to this debacle, the weapon was stuck inside the woman's head.

Cut Nose had succeeded in killing the woman instantly, as he had intended. Her praying stopped, her body went limp, and she was dead, all in the instant that she was struck. She didn't see it coming, and it is not difficult to imagine that she felt no pain at all. That was the result that Cut Nose wanted. However, he now had a problem that he had not anticipated; namely, he had the woman's limp body stuck on the end of his war club. It was as if the hole made by the war club in the woman's skull was smaller than the dimensions of the war club itself, as incredible as that might seem. The woman's body had twisted slightly as she went limp, and she might have pulled the war club from Cut Nose's hand except for the leather loop from the weapon that went around his wrist. He found himself reluctantly holding the woman up by the head.

The first couple of attempts to dislodge the weapon were gruesome failures, succeeding only in generating sloshing sounds and more splashing of brains and blood. With one hand holding the woman's bloody head by the hair, Cut Nose carefully aligned the weapon with the direction of the blow that he had delivered and, thereby, was able to extract it from the woman's skull.

This whole episode was somewhat humiliating to Cut Nose. His companions had not been very favorably impressed by their leader's efforts to show some merciful consideration to this woman as he went about killing her. Much more impressive to them was the apparent determination that Cut Nose had to kill all whites who had not already left the area. He wanted the land returned to the Dakotah people for the sole use of the Dakotah people. His companions didn't think the whites were entitled to any explanation about why it was necessary to kill them. They had laughed while Cut Nose struggled to retrieve his weapon.

"Tell her she is dead now so she must let go," one of them had joked, and the others were greatly amused by this ghoulish humor.

There would be many more whites to kill. Thinking about what had happened, Cut Nose deliberated about how to avoid the same problem in the future. He recalled having used his club to dispatch wounded deer by striking them with a well-aimed blow at the base of the skull where the head joined the neck. This had worked well many times. The club did not penetrate the animal's skull at all but caused instant death by breaking the neck and severing the brain stem. It was necessary to strike just the right spot, so the blow would have to be delivered with very great care, but that was completely in keeping with his program.

He wanted to do these things carefully. "It would be easy to kill whites this way," he thought to himself. "They don't even have antlers to get in the way."

He continued to rehearse in his mind how he would do this next time, and the more he thought about it the more convinced he became that it would work, this new method of killing. He grew anxious to give it a try.

Cut Nose did not have to wait long for an opportunity to use his war club again. And this time there was no mess at all and death came at once. He cursed himself for not having considered this method before.

The stone head of the club used by Cut Nose was shaped something like an axe head, but it was more like a hammer than an axe. It had no sharp edges. The handle was about as long as his arm. It was made out of a carefully selected branch from a butternut tree. It was very sturdy, but it had just the right amount of flexibility to give it some "snap" when striking a blow. The stone head was a triangular piece of black stone that Cut Nose had found in a dry creek bed. It was almost perfectly shaped for use as a war club when he found it. Some vigorous rubbing and scraping with another stone on both sides produced a groove where the handle could be attached. The handle was lashed to the stone with wet rawhide. When the rawhide dried, it shrank to make the lashing tight and the attachment of the handle to the stone very firm and strong enough to deliver any blow without loosening. The handle was decorated with some feathers and special beadwork and paint that identified this weapon as belonging to Cut Nose.

In addition to his war club, Cut Nose was armed with a large knife. This knife had a blade about ten inches long. It had a large bone handle that felt comfortable in Cut Nose's big hand. He also had a prized rifle with which he had hunted for a long time. He was an expert rifleman. With this rifle he could kill big game like a buffalo or a deer with one shot at more than a hundred yards. But he would use this weapon sparingly in the war against the settlers, saving his ammunition for the siege on Fort Ridgely or when attacking white communities. The siege on Fort Ridgely was already in the planning stage. His knife and war club would be sufficient for the settlers on the prairie. He could approach them as if to talk to them and then kill them before they knew what he was up to.

That is, essentially, the way it happened many times. When, as the leader of the Soldier's Lodge, he should have been working on the plans for the siege on Fort Ridgely, Cut Nose spent a lot of time that first day out on the prairie killing settlers. Perhaps he felt that he needed to be a leader in the sense of showing the others how it should be done.

Cut Nose was the leader of a war party of eight warriors including himself. He told the war party, "They must all die now or they will come back." He was not in favor of the part of the plan that allowed the whites to leave willingly. His own personal plan was to kill all the whites that he could and be done with them.

By the second day, the news had spread among the settlers that the Indians were on the warpath and many of the settlers abandoned their homesteads and headed for Fort Ridgely. Cut Nose and his party of warriors intercepted a wagon full of seven women and children on their way to Fort Ridgely, and Cut Nose personally killed them all. He did this to demonstrate his ferocious will to the members of his party. He did it to show compassion for the settlers. He wanted them to die painlessly, and he believed that he could make that happen. So he commanded his war party to stand off at about fifty yards from the wagon, to stay mounted on their horses, and to wait for his orders while he approached the wagon by himself.

The woman driving the wagon pulled up to a stop as Cut Nose neared. She could see the rest of his war party in the distance and knew that it would be futile to try to outrun them. Everyone in the wagon was terrified to the point of being speechless. Cut Nose was a large man, his face was painted black, and his body was covered with blood that he had smeared on himself. He ordered them to dismount from the wagon and make a circle around him, which they did as quickly as possible. Then he slowly turned as he talked to them, looking squarely at each one of them in turn until he had completed the circle. He told them that his people were starving and all the farmers were ruining the land. He told them that they were to blame for this and that the only way to stop these bad things from happening was for all of them to die. Then he told them to turn around and face away from the center of the circle, get on their knees, close their eyes, and pray. They all followed his orders. Nobody said anything.

Then Cut Nose commanded them, "Keep your eyes closed and do not look. Do not look!" He then proceeded to go around the circle, clubbing people once at the base of the skull, killing them instantly, one by one.

As he approached the last one, he saw that she was looking with astonishment at him and what he had done. "I warned you to not look," he shouted. "Now you suffer." He swung his war club at her hastily as she screamed hysterically. He actually wanted to kill the looker quickly to prevent further suffering, but in his haste he struck a poor blow and only succeeded in bouncing the club off the side of the woman's head, causing a severe gash which poured blood. This failed to stop her hysterical objections. He swung again, and this time the effect was an abrupt cessation of the noise and the woman's life. The silence that followed was a great relief. It signified an end to all of the present horror and was like peace. The contrast with the previous moments was surprisingly sharp.

Cut Nose stood still, his weapon poised for more action. He was not completely sure that he was finished. After the preceding flurry of activity, his own heavy breathing was all that could be heard. It was somewhat alarming to him. He seemed to return to a level of awareness that had left him while he had worked so hard and so determinedly to accomplish the job that, once started, he felt he must finish. He surveyed the scene slowly and carefully. It did appear that the work was done. He became aware that he was huffing and puffing, totally out of breath, and his face was beaded with sweat. The palms of his hands were sweaty, too, and the leather tong around his wrist from the handle of the war club had probably prevented it from flying out of his grasp.

The silence was broken by a whoop from one of the braves in the war party. All seven of them had watched from the fifty-yard distance. Now all of them approached at a gallop, and all began to whoop as they neared. Ahead of the others was Shakopee, who was almost on the ground and drawing his knife while his horse was still skidding to a halt. Before he reached the closest body Cut Nose was on him, dragging him to the ground and threatening to bash him like he had bashed the settlers.

"No!" he shouted with his teeth clenched, "You will not touch them!"

This message, it was clear, was for Shakopee and for the others as well. He stared at them all, the same determination that was there before still clearly evident on his face. Four braves were still on their horses and they remained mounted. Shakopee was quite shocked by this turn of events, but he yielded, quietly, as he got on his feet and mounted his horse. He told the others to mount up, and they did. There was a pause that seemed much longer than it actually was while Cut Nose continued to have a face to face confrontation with all seven. This ended when Shakopee wheeled his horse and whooped a happy, celebratory war cry. He kicked his horse into a gallop to the west with the others following his example, everyone echoing the whoops of Shakopee, each shout seeming to excite the others to shout and to excite the horses as well. They rode off as a group, leaving Cut Nose alone with seven dead women and children lying in the grass behind him.

Now the silence was overwhelming.

Cut Nose contemplated what he had accomplished. He had succeeded in dispatching all these people without a lot of difficulty. None of them had suffered much. His method had worked well and the whole job was a lot less gruesome than he had thought it might be. Nobody had tried to run away, perhaps because they had followed orders, kept their eyes closed, concentrated on their prayers, and did not know what was happening. Or perhaps they did know what was happening, saw others merely submitting to it, and merely followed suit. Until that last one, there had been no crying, sobbing, or screaming, and the last one didn't matter, as the others could not hear anymore. There were a few twitches and a little kicking and convulsing, but most died instantly and quietly. They did not defend themselves or try to protect one another. The children died just like the adults. The women gave them up quite easily.

Cut Nose looked over the bodies and was somewhat puzzled by the observation that these were all people whom he had never met before. At least he could not recall having seen them before, and he was always proud that he did know many of the settlers personally. Perhaps the circumstances would not allow his mind to recognize them.

No doubt the other members of his war party would have abused the bodies if Cut Nose had not stopped them. The Dakotah held certain beliefs that would have caused them to do so. For example, they believed that if the genitalia were removed from a male, then that male could not reproduce in the next life (after death). If a woman's breasts were removed from her body, she would not be able to suckle her young in the next life. Cut Nose did not allow these mutilations because he had no malice against the white people in the next life—he thought that they might have as much right to a good life there as anybody else. His main complaint against the whites was that he wanted them out of his life in this life.

On Tuesday morning, August 19, Cut Nose and his war party, which included Shakopee (Little Six), and Dowanniye, along with several other Indians, started the day by killing and mutilating four men and a woman. The men had been mowing grass, the woman raking hay. When the Indians approached, Cut Nose held out his hand to shake hands with one of the men. The man put down his scythe and shook hands, but Cut Nose then stabbed him with a knife. The man got a bear hug on Cut Nose, but the knife was still deep in his chest, Cut Nose trying hard to find something vital with it. The man bit Cut Nose on the thumb as hard as he could, trying to stop Cut Nose from doing more damage, and they both fell to the ground, with Cut Nose on the bottom. However, by now the knife had found its mark and the man went limp and rolled away, Cut Nose emerging the victor. There was a lot of blood, not only from the man, but also from Cut Nose's thumb. Cut Nose smeared his own body with blood from both sources. He then picked up the scythe that the man had been using and buried the entire long blade in the man's body. While all this was happening, the others in the war party killed the other three men and the woman and mutilated their bodies.

Just a short time later, Cut Nose's war party came upon several wagons with a party of seventeen people that included five white men, some men and a woman who were mixed-blood Indians, a full-blood Dakotah woman from the Upper Sioux Reservation, and five white women. These people knew that the war had started, and they were headed for Fort Ridgely to take refuge. They did not try to escape from Cut Nose and his party because that would not have been possible.

The warriors approached menacingly, but before any killing started, the Dakotah woman stood up and shouted at them in the Dakotah language that they were not to harm anyone. She was Mrs. Joseph R. Brown, a full-blooded Dakotah woman, wife of a white man who had served as an Indian agent at the Upper Sioux Agency. She named prominent relatives at the Upper Sioux Reservation and warned them that if anyone were harmed they would have to answer to these relatives and the whole of the Sisseton and Wahpeton tribes.

All of the members of the war party were members of the Lower Sioux Soldier's Lodge and full-blood Dakotahs who thought all whites and even half-breeds should be killed. However, this Dakotah woman was apparently quite influential. At this point, several members of the war party recognized her as Mrs. Samuel Brown, the wife of a prominent white man. She might not have been killed in any case, but what about her two half-breed sons and a daughter who were with her and the other half-breeds? The war party withdrew from the wagons to talk it over at a distance. They returned to the wagons with the intent of killing only the white men, but even that was unacceptable to Mrs. Brown, who continued to shout additional angry warnings and threats.

The war party withdrew a second time to talk it over again. The threat of losing the alliance and support of the Upper Sioux was a real possibility, according to this Sisseton woman, and the loss of their support in the uprising could not be risked. These people could be killed later, they reasoned. Very reluctantly, and with great disappointment, Cut Nose had to go along with the opinions of the others as his wish to kill the whites immediately was overwhelmingly opposed.

Returning to the wagons, the Indians let the five white men run away.[7] However, not to be put off completely, they indulged themselves sexually with the white women before accompanying the wagons back to the Lower Sioux Reservation. The members of this party were held as prisoners for the remaining duration of the war.

The Big Battles

T HE FIRST BIG BATTLE WITH WHITE SOLDIERS was hardly a battle at all, but it was the bloodiest victory in the war for the Indians. It was the ambush of a large detachment of white soldiers from Fort Ridgely in the afternoon of August 18, 1862, the first day of the uprising. When the news of the initial attack at the Lower Sioux Agency reached the fort, almost immediately after it started, the commander of the fort headed to the agency with forty-six enlisted men and an interpreter to try to learn more about the problem. When they arrived, and before they could cross the river to the agency, they were ambushed by Dakotah warriors, who killed more than one out of four of them with their first volley of fire. Some soldiers did escape, but the commander, Captain John S. Marsh, was drowned trying to escape, and more than half of his men were killed (a total of twenty-four) before the battle ended. At the outset of the war, this was a huge victory for the Indians. They lost only one man in this encounter.

The next major engagement of the war occurred the next day. Cut Nose assembled as many warriors as he could find at the reservation, perhaps as many as a hundred, and his party headed for New Ulm to begin the assault there. Very little planning went into this assault. History called it the first attack on New Ulm, which was the largest community in the area, populated by about nine hundred white folks, mostly immigrants from Germany.

With their spirits buoyed up by the successes they had experienced in killing hundreds of unsuspecting settlers across the countryside, Cut Nose and his party went at New Ulm with high expectations. They thought they would just wipe out this rather large community—plunder it, kill everyone there, and obtain a mountain of supplies for other battles. However, by this time, word of the Indian rebellion had spread. A few of the settlers had escaped the slaughter in the countryside and had alerted the New Ulm community, which responded immediately by throwing up some hasty defenses.

When Cut Nose and his warriors showed up, they were not unexpected and were met with barricades and fierce resistance. The Indians managed to burn a few of the outlying buildings, but they were held off from making a major assault on the town's main defenses. They could see that they would need a larger force and some strategic planning to take this community. They accomplished very little except to confirm for the townspeople that a war with the Indians had begun. Six of the citizens of New Ulm were killed and five more were wounded, but those numbers were nothing compared to what the Indians had thought they would do. Having arrived too late in the day to accomplish much more, the Indians withdrew at nightfall to return to the reservation.

Just as the Indians were getting ready to pull out, however, they managed to ambush a party of sixteen men in wagons and on horseback. These men had left New Ulm early in the day to scout the area south and west of the town. Unfortunately for them, on their way back they ran right into Cut Nose and his large war party of Indians, who had seen them coming and were lying in ambush. Five members of the scouting party managed to get through, but the other eleven were killed. From the Indians' point of view, this was a relatively successful engagement, a victory of sorts for the Indians, who suffered no casualties at all. Nevertheless, on the way home they were quite disappointed about the action at New Ulm. They were very tired, and wet from a late-afternoon thunderstorm, and their mood leaving was much more subdued than it had been on their approach to New Ulm.

When they arrived at the reservation, they learned that preparations were being made for a major assault on Fort Ridgely. The reservation was full of warriors who had returned from the scattered assaults made on the settlers across the countryside. The mood among these celebrating warriors was still buoyed from the successes they had experienced in the slaughter of the farmers. They just laughed when they heard about the foray that Cut Nose had led against New Ulm. They chided and scolded him for having gone off to make this attack without enough planning or preparation or force.

In the context of all their recent victories with almost no casualties at all, the other warriors could scarcely believe Cut Nose when he told them of the defenses at New Ulm and the resistance he had encountered. Besides, there were now hundreds of additional warriors assembled at the Lower Sioux reservation. They had come from other reservations and gathered at Lower Sioux to participate in the assault on Fort Ridgely, which now was planned for the next day. They, too, had swept through the countryside wiping out the settlers along their way. They, too, were in a mood for celebrating their victories. Nobody wanted to hear about the relative failure that Cut Nose had experienced at New Ulm.

Plenty of whiskey, appropriated from the stores of the settlers, added to the jubilant mood. Many of the Indians became quite drunk, not only from the whiskey, but also from the elation resulting from their successful battles. The celebrating went on well into the night. There was a lot of eating and drinking and whooping and hollering and storytelling and drunken laughter. Although they were supposed to be planning their strategy for a major battle the next day, not much energy was devoted to that. The opinion was widely held that not much strategy would be needed as the Fort would be simply overwhelmed, and there would not be much of a battle required to take it as it would not be well defended. Furthermore, it was believed that once the Fort was taken, the whites would abandon the community of New Ulm and all of the rest of the territory south of the big cities to the north, Minneapolis and St Paul.

The march of the Indians to Fort Ridgely the next morning started later than was first anticipated. Because of the celebrating in the night, some preparations were neglected until morning and had to be completed before the march could begin. Some of the warriors were still drunk, and many had serious hangovers. As a result, Little Crow could muster only about 400 warriors for the battle, although many more were present in the vicinity. They did not arrive at Fort Ridgely until early afternoon.

The Indians had no way of knowing it, but had Cut Nose decided to attack Fort Ridgely instead of New Ulm the previous afternoon, he actually might have won that battle. The garrison at the fort had been small to begin with, but it was seriously depleted by the loss of most of the company that was ambushed by the Indians at the Redwood ferry on the first day of the uprising. By the time the eventual attack on Fort Ridgely was initiated, the garrison had been significantly reinforced. Help had arrived from several sources, including the forty-five "Renville Rangers," the company of half-breeds that the Indians had believed had left to fight in the Civil War. Now there was a force of well over 200 armed men to help defend the fort.

The fort was actually not well fortified. It had the defensive advantage of being located on high ground, but there was no wall, stockade, fence, or other obstacle surrounding it. It consisted only of a cluster of buildings including a large barracks for the men, several buildings for officers' quarters, a headquarters building, a commissary, and other buildings in the surrounding area which were stables, storehouses, a hospital, a granary, and other minor support buildings. Many buildings were crowded with settlers, approximately 200 of them, who escaped the onslaught of the Indians and came to the fort seeking refuge.

The attack strategy that was developed by the Indians was for Chief Little Crow and a group of warriors to create a diversionary action against the west side of the fort while the main body of the forces would approach from the northeast. This strategy succeeded to the extent that the Indians in the main force were able to reach some of the outbuildings on the northeast corner of the fort and inflict some casualties there. However, Little Crow was wounded in the diversionary action, and cannon fire from the fort rattled the Indians to such an extent that they retreated from the ground they had gained and took cover in a nearby ravine. One witness later said that the cannon fire had "mortally frightened" the Indians. The Indians clearly had not anticipated cannon fire. Most had never before encountered it. There were only three cannons at the fort, but they were used effectively, even if they did not inflict large numbers of casualties among the Indians.

For the rest of the day, the battle continued at long range. The Indians lobbed rifle shots at the fort ineffectively, and the garrison in the fort fired their cannon occasionally, with just enough frequency to keep the Indians at bay. This went on for several hours until the weather intervened, and rain began to fall. The enthusiasm of the Indians for the attack was thoroughly dampened by the rain, especially compounded by the cannon fire and nightfall. A wounded Chief Little Crow and the whole Indian attack force withdrew once again to the reservation. The warriors were tired. Some hadn't slept for days. This first siege on the fort ended much like the attack on New Ulm had ended. It was the second botched engagement in two days, a very disappointing failure for the Indians.

It rained all of the next day, and the Indians needed the time to rest and recuperate and think about what had gone wrong at Fort Ridgely and at New Ulm. There was no more celebrating. Things were not going well anymore, and the dreams of taking Fort Ridgely and New Ulm with ease had vanished. It was evident to the leaders that stronger leadership was needed; they could not have their warriors going off pell-mell across the countryside anymore just firing at will at the white populace. Some organized and concerted efforts would be required to accomplish the bigger victories they wanted. It would not be correct to say that they were reorganizing, because up to now they had been quite disorganized. However, they now began to get organized. Part of the day was devoted to planning the next assault on Fort Ridgely. They would assemble a larger force of men who were better prepared to make the siege that would be necessary.

While this planning was going on, however, the white defenders were not just sitting on their thumbs. The water supply at the fort was replenished. There was no well there, and water had to be carried from a distance. Some barricades were strengthened, and better defense strategies were devised. The cannons were strategically placed to provide even more effective fire. The soldiers and armed civilians at the fort were given assignments that would provide better defense.

At New Ulm, the same things were happening. Reinforcements for the defense of the town were arriving from several sources. Many volunteers from settlements east of New Ulm arrived. Sturdier barricades were constructed, and parts of the town were evacuated so that the defenses could be concentrated in a more secure area. As a result of the rainy one-day interlude in the fighting, the Indians' chances of taking either the fort or the town of New Ulm had diminished, despite their improved organization and their rest and recuperation.

The next day the Indians made their second attempt to take Fort Ridgely. This time they had a force estimated at twice the number present in the first attack. Perhaps as many as eight hundred Indians from several tribes showed up to lay siege to the fort, but again the action didn't start until mid-afternoon. They launched volleys of flaming arrows to set fires, but that was not effective because of the recent rain. They tried to use some of the abandoned outbuildings for cover, but cannon fire from the main part of the fort set those buildings afire. The cannons continued to play a major role in repelling the Indians as they were aimed for point-blank fire when the Indians charged the fort. At the end of the day, the casualties within the fort were light—only three killed and thirteen wounded. Casualties among the Indians were estimated to be much higher, although years later the Indians themselves claimed that only two were killed. In any case, the resistance from the fort was sufficient to cause the Indians to back off.

Retreating again from the stiff resistance and cannon fire that came from the fort, the Indians diverted their efforts to regroup and proceed on to New Ulm. Unaware that this community was now well reinforced with hundreds of armed men east of the town who had come to help in its defense, the Indians were confident that they could overwhelm the community with their large force. By now they were frustrated and angry and in need of a victory to bolster their confidence. They were desperate to have a victory at New Ulm, and the battle that began the next morning reflected their determination.

It started at about 9:30 with a horde of warriors charging the town from the west. They came at the town yelling ferociously, causing the defenders stationed at the western perimeter to retreat immediately. The Indians quickly occupied some of the outbuildings and surrounded the town's main defenses, but they could not penetrate the barricades and were suffering significant losses resulting from snipers located at strategic points in the town's defenses.

The Indians made several attempts to breach the barricades, but all were unsuccessful. When one of their charges in mid-afternoon was met with a counter charge of riflemen from behind the barricades, the tide of the whole battle turned, putting the defenders in control. That night the New Ulm defenders set fire to all of the outbuildings occupied by the Indians. The next morning, there was a lot of open space that the Indians needed to cross before they could get close enough to make their rifle fire effective. The Indians were still around in the morning, and they lobbed a few long-distance, ineffective shots at the defenders, but then they withdrew. The battle was essentially over. In fact, the war was essentially over.

Although there would be other battles, some quite bloody, the outcome of the whole 1862 Sioux Indian Uprising was already determined. A force of fourteen hundred well-armed soldiers were on their way to Fort Ridgely. They would arrive there within two days. Unable to take the fort, and unable to take New Ulm, the Indians had to know that their dreams of taking the land back from the white man were not going to be completely realized. But they had already taken back some of the land from the settlers, and perhaps they thought they could hang on to that. At least, they could defensively resist any efforts of the white man to recapture it. It didn't occur to them that their efforts to rid the countryside of whites might backfire and that the Indians could end up being the ones who would be evicted.

The next major encounter was a notable victory for the Indians. On August 31, a week after the second attack on the town of New Ulm, a party of about 170 men set out from Fort Ridgely to find out what the Dakotah were up to, and where they were. A third of this force was mounted, the rest in wagons or on foot. They headed west from the fort toward the Lower Sioux reservation, stopping intermittently to bury the many victims of the Dakotah they found along the way. After two days in the field, they had encountered no Indians and concluded that they had left the area. However, the Indians were still active in the countryside, and some Indian scouts had spotted them and learned the location of their camp.

Just before dawn on the third day, the soldiers were awakened by gunfire. The Indians had surrounded their camp during the night. The Indians were led by Chief Big Eagle, who has been described as "the best warrior on either side." Cut Nose is not mentioned in conjunction with this battle, known as the Battle of Birch Coulee. Where he was at the time is not known, but he was likely still out prowling the countryside and attacking settlers. Chief Big Eagle had opposed the war, but once the fighting started, he led his men against the soldiers and didn't allow them to attack white settlements. The Indians began the attack while most of the soldiers were still sleeping. Thirty or more of the soldiers were shot during the first few minutes. Heavy fighting continued for an hour and then tapered off, though some exchange of fire continued through the day.

Relief came in the morning of the following day when artillery came from Fort Ridgely and, once again, the Indians were dispersed by cannon fire. Of the original party of soldiers, thirteen had been killed, forty-seven seriously wounded, and many more of them less seriously injured. All ninety of their horses were dead. This battle was a victory for the Indians who suffered few casualties, perhaps only two killed. After the failures at New Ulm and Fort Ridgely, this battle raised Indian spirits enough to initiate at least two more attacks on white fortifications, but that wouldn't change the final outcome. The next engagements failed much like those previous battles at Fort Ridgely and New Ulm, and then many of the Indians, including Cut Nose, surrendered.

Prior to the surrender, the Indians had such severe disagreement among themselves over whether they should continue fighting that they came close to fighting with each other. There were many who had opposed fighting the whites since before the war began. These were called the "friendlies." Those who supported the war and did the actual fighting were called the "hostiles." At the end of the war, the "friendlies" got organized at a camp they established, which eventually became known as Camp Release near what is now the town of Montevideo. This name was the apparent result of the eventual release of 259 captives (107 whites and 152 with mixed blood) whom the Indians had been holding prisoner. Prior to the actual surrender of all the Indians, the friendlies actually tried to hide many of the white and mixed-blood captives taken by the hostiles. This was done to protect those captives from being killed by the hostiles. All during the captivity of the whites and mixed bloods, the hostiles threatened to kill them. It was the friendlies who began to communicate with the white soldiers about ending the war.

Rather than surrender, some of the hostiles ran off without being captured, escaping with their families to North Dakota or Canada. Little Crow and some of the other leaders of the uprising got away in this manner when it became clear that the vast majority of the hostiles in the vicinity did not wish to continue with the war. Some hostiles joined the friendlies at Camp Release. The friendlies were now in control and were making the major decisions in the negotiations for ending the war. All the Indians in the camp peacefully surrendered to the soldiers when they arrived and took over. Then the hostiles, numbering more than 400, were required to turn in their weapons and were soon separated from the friendlies and held as prisoners under close guard. All of these were soon brought to trial before a military commission.

Chapter Six

ɛ♦ɔ

The Trials and the Hanging Preparations

T HE WAR WAS NOW OVER, barely five weeks after it had begun. Hundreds of settlers, perhaps as many as six hundred in all, had been killed, most of them in the wanton slaughter that the Indians inflicted on the white farmers and their families in the first two days of the uprising. By comparison, the actual battles of the war resulted in relatively few casualties, with the Indians suffering fewer casualties than the whites. However, the white soldiers were more organized and just kept coming on with more and more reinforcements. It became clear to the Indians that they had underestimated the white forces, just as Chief Little Crow had warned them in the beginning. The whites being victorious, the Indians would now be required to atone for their wrongdoings and would be subjected to some kind of punishment.

The "trials" of the Indians began within days of their capture. A military tribunal was assembled to determine who, among all of the prisoners, were actually guilty of active participation in the uprising, who had killed the white settlers and fought the battles with the soldiers. A review of the handwritten transcripts of these trials is very revealing. For some of the Indian defendants there were very specific charges and specifications made against them. In most cases, however, the charges and specifications were quite general and simply repeated from one trial to the next.

For example, the very first of the captives to be tried was Otakle, a half-breed of a different sort, with Negro and white ancestry, who became an informant for the white tribunal. In all the subsequent trials, he spoke freely about how each of the captives brought before the tribunal had participated in the uprising. He was charged with murdering seven white people (and found not guilty, despite his confession during the hearing). Most, if not nearly all, of the defendants, however, had general charges and specifications worded almost exactly alike as follows:

> Charge: Participation in the murders, robberies, and outrages committed by the Sioux Indians on the Minnesota Frontier.

> Specifications: In this that said [name], a Sioux Indian, did join with and participate in the murders, robberies and outrages committed by the Sioux Tribe of Indians on the Minnesota Frontier between the 18th day of August 1862 and the 28th day of September 1862 . . .

If it were known that a specific individual had been present at certain battles, then the specifications might also list the battles in which the defendant participated.

The trials were interrupted soon after they started when all of the captives were moved from Camp Release to the Lower Sioux Agency. There they resumed, each captive being tried individually. Each one would have an appearance before the tribunal and was allowed to make a statement. Some freely admitted to what they had done in the war, but others said they had done nothing against the whites. The informant, Otakle, did not always agree with what the captives had to say. Many of the trials were completed in about five minutes. The tribunal sentenced to death all of those who admitted that they had been active participants in the war or who were found guilty of having participated even if they didn't admit it. The informant's recollections carried a great deal of weight in these decisions. It is noteworthy that in one case there was no testimony at all reflected by the transcript of the trial except for the defendant's denial of the general charge and specifications. Nevertheless, this defendant was found guilty and sentenced to be hanged.

The trials of all hostiles were completed in less than six weeks. In this short period of time, 392 Indians were tried. Three hundred seven Indians were sentenced to death, and it was the intentions of the white captors to hang all of them. Another sixteen Indians were sentenced to go to prison. The whites were so angry and so full of hatred for the Indians that if they could have conceived of a reasonable justification for it, even if contrived, they might have hanged all two thousand of their captives, including all the old folks, women, and children.

As soon as the trials were over, all of the captives who were not condemned to death were relocated to Fort Snelling. Numbering approximately 1,700, they started out on foot and in wagons in a procession four miles long. The arduous trip would take several days. Along the way the Indians suffered brutal treatment from their white captors. Near the halfway mark, at Henderson, the angry citizens brutalized them as they passed through the town. The soldiers escorting the Indians tried to protect them, but they could not protect them all. Many were beaten or otherwise severely abused by the citizens of Henderson. A white woman pulled a baby from its mother's arms and threw the hapless child to the ground. What horror could the white woman have experienced to motivate such an atrocity? The mother retrieved the child, but it died hours later. This child was lovingly laid to rest in a tree, well beyond the town after all the Indians had passed through and made camp for the night. This Indian-style burial is said to have been the last of that kind to take place in Minnesota, although that is doubtful because there were many more deaths to follow.

Another example of the extreme anger and hatred that the whites had for the Indians at this time was observed a month later when 303 condemned captives were relocated from the Lower Sioux Agency to the vicinity of Mankato, a distance of about sixty miles. All of them were bound and put in wagons and hauled directly through the town of New Ulm. While passing through the town the captives were stoned and pummeled mercilessly by the angry citizens. The soldiers escorting the Indians tried, probably passively, to protect their captives, but they did not succeed in doing that. The beatings were so severe that some of the Indians died as a result.

On November 9 they arrived at Mankato. All the condemned Indians were lodged at a place called "Camp Lincoln" located at the west edge of the town (in South Bend). There they were to wait to be hanged. But many things happened before the hangings could actually take place. As time passed following the end of the war, people began to think more calmly about what was happening, especially regarding the hanging of 303 Indians. The people in charge hesitated and even questioned their own legal authority to hang such a large number of Indians. They appealed to the president of the United States to affirm their authority to do this.

This hesitation was frustrating to many of the local citizens, who wanted to get on with the hanging and get it over with. On December 4, four weeks had passed since the Indians had arrived at Camp Lincoln and still not even one of the Indians had been hung. On this date, a large group of citizens, approximately 200 of them, emboldened by a lot of liquor, decided that they were tired of waiting for the soldiers to do the job. With lynching on their minds, they headed out to Camp Lincoln to do it themselves. However, when they got there, the calmer and more sober heads of the soldiers guarding the camp prevailed. There was a confrontation between the mob and the soldiers, but the citizens were turned away without a battle. The very next day, the Indians were moved to more secure quarters. A large jail had been prepared in Mankato near the site where the hanging was to take place. There the condemned Indians could be more assuredly protected.

One day after that, a letter arrived from Abraham Lincoln himself. He had rejected the proposition that 303 Indians should be hanged and reduced the number to thirty-nine, listing in his own handwriting the names of the prisoners to be hanged. In doing this, he was caught between the proverbial rock and a hard place. He knew that many people were going to be disappointed no matter what he decided, as he had received appeals for clemency for the Indians as well as appeals opposed to any clemency for them.[8] He asked two of his staff to search through all the trial transcripts of the 303 Indians who were condemned to death, instructing them to pick out the ones who had sexually violated their captive white women. The number produced by this initial search was only two, to the great surprise of the president. He had been told that more than a hundred white women had been captured and nearly all of them had been violated. Surely it would have taken more than two Indians to accomplish that kind of sexual rampage.

President Lincoln asked his staff to review the trial transcripts a second time, this time selecting those who had participated in massacres as opposed to having merely participated in a battle during the uprising. How he defined a "massacre" is not known, but this search produced a list of forty Indians which included the two who had committed sexual crimes. A review of what is known about the war activities of some of those selected is enough to suggest that the judgments of the president's staff in the making of this list were questionable, although Cut Nose certainly belonged on the list and his name was there. Lincoln noted that one of the names on the list of forty, Otakle, was recommended by the tribunal for clemency, and the President left his name off the list of those to be hanged, yielding a final list of thirty-nine Indians whom he ordered to be hanged.

While all of this was happening, the many preparations for the hanging were being completed. Obviously, when the time came for building the scaffold to hang the Indians, the plan was to hang a lot of them. Initially, over three hundred had been sentenced by the military tribunal to be put to death. The popular sentiment among the local civilians was to go on from there and hang every Indian they could find. If there was any truth to the belief widely held by the Indians before the war that the whites were out to exterminate all of them, much more evidence could be found for that belief now. Apparently, most of the whites did believe that the only good Indian was a dead one. In any case, if all those 303 Indians were to be hanged, some special equipment would be needed. It would take a very long time to hang them all one at a time, so a scaffold was built that could hang groups of forty simultaneously.

Materials for building the scaffold were a concern for a time—they would be needed right away and were not readily available. Some extra large timbers would be needed, as well as a lot of rope. Fortunately, a local farmer had recently planned to build a new barn and had placed an order for some big timbers to be shipped from a mill over by the Big Woods area near the Mississippi River. The Army could commandeer these timbers temporarily for use in this mass hanging.

The scaffold was a major construction effort for a period of time. The framework was made out of large oak timbers, and it resembled the framework for a new barn or other building that would be fairly large—bigger than most houses built at this time. It was square, about thirty feet long on each side, and about fifteen feet high. The four corner posts were set into the ground and then a post was set into the ground in the middle of each side. Beams that ran from one post to the next at the top tied all the posts together.

These crossbeams were the same kind of sturdy oak timbers that made the vertical support posts. Each would have to span fifteen feet and support the weight of five Indians. Ten Indians could be hanged on each side of the square scaffold. At the exact center of the scaffold structure, where lines from each corner would cross, a very long and exceptionally large pole was set deep into the ground. This pole rose to a height much higher than the sides of the scaffold, perhaps thirty feet. The pole itself was straight and true, a carefully trimmed and debarked trunk of a large evergreen tree, perhaps a northern red or white pine. It would be the main support for the suspended platform on which the forty Indians would stand as they were about to be hanged. Ropes that ran up to a sturdy steel retaining ring around the top of the center pole would suspend this platform. The whole mechanism was designed so that when the rope holding the retaining ring was cut, the weight of the suspended platform would cause it to fall out from under the Indians and crash to the ground, leaving the Indians suspended in the air by the ropes around their necks.

By the time the hangings were to get started, the scaffold had been ready for several days. Lincoln's letter had limited the number of Indians to be hanged to thirty-nine, but even so, there was still not enough rope available to hang thirty-nine Indians at one time. A lot of the available rope had been used in the making of the extra heavy-duty ropes needed to suspend the platform. The kind of heavy rope needed for that purpose was not generally available, and a lot of small ropes were braided together and used up in the making of the big heavy-duty ropes needed to suspend not only the platform but also the thirty-eight Indians who would be standing on it. Consequently, there was a shortage of rope for the purpose of making the actual nooses needed to string up the Indians. A lot of rope was required. More than three feet of rope was required just to tie it to the large beam. Another couple of feet would be needed for the noose at the other end. With a few feet of distance between the beam and the noose, they needed at least ten feet of rope per Indian, and they were planning to hang forty of them, so that's 400 feet of rope. They just didn't have that much on hand, so the date for the hangings to begin was delayed for one week, postponed from December 19 to December 26, the day after Christmas.

Getting the rope needed was an incredible problem, however. Rope was a highly valued commodity among farmers and the local farmers quickly bought up every load of rope that was shipped in by the local merchants. There was very little on hand. The Army went out to get all the rope they could from all the local farmers, all they could spare. In this manner, a lot of rope was obtained, but the farmers kept their best ropes for their own use—they depended heavily on this commodity for many purposes. The ropes donated were the old ones, the unreliable frayed ones, the ones that had been left out in the rain lying on the ground, the rotten ones. They needed their good ropes and kept them.

When enough rope was gathered, forty nooses were fashioned and tied to the supporting beams of the scaffold. Notches were cut into the support beams so that there would be no sharp corners that could possibly damage the ropes or even sever them. With this accomplished, all was in readiness for the hanging.

This was not going to be the usual way to hang somebody. Ordinarily, a hanging platform is high enough so that, when the trap was sprung, the person being hanged fell a few feet before coming to the end of his rope with a sudden stop several feet above the ground. With that kind of hanging, the victim's neck was usually broken by the fall and death was almost instantaneous.

At least, the victim would lose consciousness right away. With that method, the victim died quickly, mercifully, and didn't suffer very much.

The way these Indians were to be hanged, however, they would suffer. There was no sudden drop, no fall. There was no sudden stop at the end of the rope, so their necks were not broken. The rope was already fairly snug around their necks when the floor fell away from under them; when they lost the support beneath their feet they were already very near the end of their rope. The ropes around their necks simply tightened and held them suspended in air, causing them to strangle. They were conscious when that happened. They felt it happen. They lost consciousness slowly. When the noose tightened around the neck, they could not cry out or complain. Their hands were tied and their arms shackled behind their backs, and they could only kick. Perhaps they kept kicking reflexively even after losing consciousness. Mercifully, this kicking would serve to tighten the ropes around their necks even more and, thereby, bring death to end their suffering somewhat more quickly. But it was a horrible way to go, and nobody would choose to go like that. Nobody would think it was merciful, and it was very possible that the local folks had all this figured out and were not interested in being merciful. That's how deep their hatred ran.

Of the thirty-nine names listed by Lincoln, only the sentence of one, Round Wind, was commuted. All the remaining thirty-eight were hanged at 10:15 a.m. on December 26, 1862, in the largest simultaneous public execution ever to take place in American history.

The names of Indians are sometimes difficult to translate to English. For that matter, they are sometimes difficult to translate to the written Dakotah language, also, because the Dakotah had no written language. As a consequence, attempts to record the spoken word or even the oral sounds of the Dakotah language sometimes do not work well. There are at least three dialects in the Sioux language—Dakotah, Lakotah, and Nakotah. These correspond to the Santee, Teton, and Yankton branches of the Sioux Nation respectively.

Attempts to write Indian expressions (names included) amounted to approximating the Indian sounds with a phonetic record. Some of the actual sounds were not easy to record even with this phonetic system, so only an approximation of the sounds was possible. This imperfect method of recording resulted in small variations being common for the spelling of a single name or expression. For example, Dowansa was one of the thirty-eight hanged. The name, "Dowansa," translates to English as, "The Singer." But this name might be seen variously spelled as Do-wan-sa (to emphasize that this is a phonetic interpretation of a Sioux name), or Do-WAN-sa (to indicate that the second syllable is emphasized in the pronunciation), or even Do-WAN-sah, with the "h" added according to the perception of the interpreter.

Round Wind, Ta-te-mi-ma, had been convicted of murder and the capture of women and children. He was an old man, a brother-in-law of Joseph Renville who was a well-known trader in the area even forty years before the start of the war. Round Wind had been the public crier for Little Crow before and during the massacre, but after the battle of Wood Lake, near the end of the war, he joined the antiwar group, the friendlies, and was their public crier at Camp Release, when the captives were freed. He was the only one of the thirty-nine in Lincoln's list who had regularly attended Protestant worship even long before the uprising. A few days before he knew that he was one of those to be hanged, he had professed repentance and faith in Christ and had been baptized. He had been convicted by the testimony of two German boys who said they saw him kill their mother. He strenuously denied the accusation.

Dr. Williamson, Round Wind's minister, took up his case after his trial and conviction and after he was sentenced to be hanged. Williamson was able to demonstrate that the accusing boys were mistaken. On the day he was accused of having committed the murder, Round Wind was many miles away helping some whites to escape. Some of those whom he had helped submitted statements that it was impossible for Round Wind to have done the murder. Dr. Williamson sent this evidence at once to President Lincoln. With only a few hours to spare before the execution would take place, Lincoln telegraphed a reprieve. For the rest of his life the old man named Round Wind attributed his rescue from the gallows to the direct intervention of God. With Round Wind's last-minute reprieve, thirty-eight remained on President Lincoln's handwritten list.

O-ta-kle (Many Kills), alias Joseph Godfrey, a mulatto Negro, was engaged extensively in the massacre. His mother was black, his father French-Canadian. He was married to a Dakotah woman. He had lived at the Lower Agency for five years. He was the very first to be tried by the military commission. He was charged with murdering seven white men and generally participating in the uprising. During his hearing by the commission, he actually admitted to having killed seven white men. A woman who had survived captivity by the Indians and who had been taken prisoner by Otakle testified that he boasted to her of having killed seventeen whites. Incredibly, despite the testimony of this woman and his own confession, he was found not guilty of murdering the seven white men, but he was convicted of having participated in all the major battles of the uprising. He was initially sentenced to hang, but because he turned states' evidence he was given clemency, and his sentence was commuted to ten years in prison. He served three years, was released, and then lived with the Dakotah at Niobrara, Nebraska, where he farmed industriously until he died in 1909.

Sketch of the hanging of the thirty-eight Indians in Mankato, Minnesota. (Courtesy of the Blue Earth County Historical Society)

Chapter Eight

ಬ ♦ ಚಿ

The Thirty-Eight Hanged

THE NAMES OF THOSE WHO WERE HANGED are listed below: (The names are spelled phonetically exactly as they were in the list that was handwritten by Abraham Lincoln.)[9]

Te-he-hdo-ne-cha (One Who Forbids His House): He was convicted of taking a white woman prisoner, raping her, and being otherwise engaged in the massacre.

Ta-zoo, or Tazu, (Old Buffalo), alias Plan-doo-ta (Red Otter): He was charged with abetting the murder of a trader and raping a young girl, Mattie Williams, and participating in other crimes. He testified that for a long time he had such sore eyes that he couldn't even hunt, so he couldn't have killed anybody. Regarding the accusation of rape, he claimed that he was a professional juggler and that a young girl came to him, but he denied that he raped her. However, the girl testified in person that he did indeed rape her and that he also was in the war party that killed a trader. Her testimony was backed up by the testimony of another woman who witnessed the incident.

Wy-a-the-to-wah (His People): He was charged with and convicted of participating in the murder of a white trader. During his hearing before the commission he admitted that he had shot at the trader, but he said, "I don't know whether I hit him or not." He also admitted to having fired shots at the battles of New Ulm, Birch Coolie, and Wood Lake.

Hin-han-shoon-ko-yag (One Who Walks Clothed in an Owl's Tail): He was convicted of the murder of Alexander Hunter and taking Mrs. Hunter prisoner. At his hearing he denied killing the man, but Mrs. Hunter testified that she saw him shoot her husband at a range of three feet and that she then had to talk him out of cutting her husband's throat. He took Mrs. Hunter to Chief Little Crow's village as his prisoner. He admitted at his hearing that he took part in a battle at Fort Ridgely and one at Wood Lake.

Muz-za-bom-a-du (Iron Blower): He was convicted of the murder of an old woman and a child. At his hearing he admitted being at the place where a white trader was killed, but he said, "I have not shot or killed a white man." He said that he heard shots being fired, but he was not with the war party. Otakle, the mulatto who turned states' evidence, testified that the old man did kill an old woman and her child. Iron Blower denied this allegation but was found guilty nonetheless.

Wah-pay-du-ta (Red Leaf): He was found guilty of shooting a white man. He was an old man. He admitted that he shot at the man through a window, but he did not think he killed him. He also admitted he was wounded while participating in an attack at New Ulm. David Faribault, a half-breed, testified at this hearing and stated, "All the Dakotas have killed whites. If the guilty are punished there will be none left."

Wa-he-hua (Meaning of name unknown): He was convicted of murder. He admitted to having been in three battles and having shot at white people, but he added, "I never took good aim." He also claimed that the warriors in the Soldier's Lodge made him go with them. David Faribault testified that he heard the defendant tell another Indian that he shot a white man off a horse, wounding him, and then he shot the white man dead. The defendant claimed that Faribault lied, that he did not kill anybody, and that if he had killed any white man he would have fled with Little Crow instead of surrendering.

Qua-ma-ni (Tinkling Walker): He was convicted of the murder of two persons. His conviction resulted from the testimony of two German boys.

He claimed that the boys were mistaken, as he was not at the place of the murder at all.

Rda-in-yan-kua (Rattling Runner): He participated actively in the New Ulm battle. He claimed that the Soldier's Lodge was forcing others to join them in the war. He denied the charge against him but admitted he was opposed to the delivery of the captives to the friendly Indians. Again, David Faribault, a half-breed, gave testimony that hurt Rattling Runner's defense. Faribault testified that Rattling Runner took a prominent role in many battles, giving rousing speeches to the war parties and leading the way in battles. A son-in-law of Chief Wabasha, he wrote a very bitter but eloquent letter to Chief Wabasha just before he was hanged. The text of his letter is worth passing along:

> Wabasha, you have deceived me. You told me that if we followed the advice of General Sibley, and give ourselves up to the whites, all would be well; no innocent man would be injured. I have not killed, wounded, or injured a white man, or any white persons. I have not participated in the plunder of their property; and yet to-day I am set apart for execution, and must die in a few days, while men who are guilty will remain in prison. My wife is your daughter, my children are your grandchildren. I leave them in your care and under your protection. Do not let them suffer; and when my children are grown up, let them know that their father died because he followed the advice of his chief, and without having the blood of a white man to answer for to the Great Spirit.[10]

Do-wan-sa (The Singer): Convicted of murdering a woman in the Swan Lake neighborhood and of attempting to ravish her daughter. Another Indian killed the daughter before Dowansa could accomplish the rape. He admitted being present when his companions killed two white men and two white women, but he denied that he took any part.

Ha-pan (Second Child, if a Son): Participated in the murder of a trader and took Mrs. Williams prisoner. He admitted he was present when the trader was killed, but claimed another Indian did the killing. He also admitted that he took Mrs. Williams as a prisoner. During his hearing he also said, "I have been in all the fights. I don't remember of killing a white man."

Shoon-ka-ska (White Dog): He was charged with participating in the uprising, the specifications stating that he gave the command to fire on Captain Marsh and his party when they were ambushed by the Indians. He was found guilty of leading the ambush at the Lower Agency ferry, when Captain Marsh and more than half his command were killed. He claimed the whites misunderstood his action on this occasion, and that he was for peace and did not give the signal for the Indians to fire on Captain Marsh and his men as he was accused of having done. Since 1851, when the Indians still lived at Kaposia, an old village located at what is now South St Paul, White Dog was prominent among the group of Indians who were farmers. When the Indians moved to the Lower Agency, near Morton, after the treaties of 1851 and 1857, White Dog was known as the most accomplished farmer at the agency. In fact, he was a leader in the "improvement band" or "pantaloon band," a group of farmer Indians that was causing Little Crow some concern because this group was attracting more and more of his warriors. Even many of his close relatives were becoming farmers and increasingly friendly with the whites. In this context, White Dog's denial that he participated in the ambush of the soldiers had more credibility, but he was hanged nevertheless.

Toon-kan-e-chah-tah-mane (One Who Walks by His Grandfather): He was convicted of the murder of a man in a wagon and of participating otherwise in the massacre. He claimed that another Indian did the killing in question and that the only wrong he did was to take a blanket from one of the stores at the Lower Agency. He admitted that he had been at the battles of Fort Ridgely and New Ulm, but he denied that he fired his gun.

E-tay-hoo-tay (Red Face): Convicted of murdering Mr. George Washington Divoll at the start of the uprising. In addition, on the basis of testimony from David Faribault, he was found guilty of killing seven other white persons on the north side of the Minnesota River, and also the murder of another man and woman. He denied the charges but admitted being present when murders were committed. Faribault testified, "He told me he killed Divoll."

Am-da-cha (Broken to Pieces): He was convicted of taking David Faribault prisoner and killing two persons at Faribault's house. David

Faribault testified that he did that. Broken to Pieces said that he didn't remember doing that. He admitted that he went with hostile Indians to a battle at Fort Ridgely and to the battle at Wood Lake and shot his gun off twice at both places, but he did not think he killed anyone. He also admitted that he took some goods from Forbes' (one of the traders) store.

Hay-pee-don (Third Child, if a Son): He was found guilty of cutting Mrs. Thieler with a hatchet and engaging in the massacre. He admitted being in three of the battles and firing his gun six times, and that he captured a woman and two children, and that he stole two horses. It should be noted that some Indians made this kind of confession with the expectation that they would be treated as prisoners of war. They did not expect that a confession of this kind would be tantamount to signing their own death warrants. However, any Indian who actively participated in the fighting was sentenced to hang.

Mahpe-o-ke-na-ji (Who Stands on a Cloud, "Cut Nose"): He was accused of the murder of Antoine Young and a white man and woman. He denied the charge but admitted to having fired his gun a few times. It was proven after the trials that he had killed nineteen women and children in a wagon by braining them with his tomahawk.

At his hearing before the military tribunal, Cut Nose acknowledged having been at several of the major battles during the uprising, but he said that he did not kill a white man at any time. However, one witness testified that he saw Cut Nose level his gun at Antoine Young and fire. Another witness testified that Cut Nose and forty warriors made an attack on settlers in a wagon at Redwood, saying, "He shot a man off a wagon. I saw him strike the persons in the wagon with a knife. There were four women and eleven children. They were all killed."

His Indian name, Mahpeokenaji, means "Who Stands on a Cloud" in the Dakotah language. The Dakotah name given to Cut Nose as a baby stood out from other names, truly an enviable one. "Who Stands on a Cloud" may be the equivalent of "Angel." That's a great name, one that occurs commonly among Hispanic people today. If one of his companions on the gallows could be named Wakantonka ("Great Spirit"), then it is not so unusual that Cut Nose had a name similar to "Angel."

Among all the other Indians who eventually died with Cut Nose there were some with names that were relatively easy to imagine, in terms of how they might have been acquired. The imagination is not stretched far when envisioning what the stimulus for these names might have been, and some were not very imaginative at all. Hay-pee-don (Third Child, if a son) is a good example. Wah-pay-du-ta (Red Leaf) is another.

"Who Stands on a Cloud" is a much more curious name, however, even for an Indian. How could such a name be given? Was an angel present at his birth? Would that name make Cut Nose someone special even from birth? A name like that could effect his life, his self-concept, even if the name only gave him reason to think that he might be someone special. In many ways, he was someone special. It is well documented that he did a lot of killing during the uprising even if some of the stories about his killing were exaggerations. In that activity, he was, indeed, an angel, but an angel of death.

Henry Milord, a half-breed: He was accused of participating in the murder of a white man. He was a bright young man, who had been brought up in the home of General Sibley. He pleaded not guilty to the charges against him. He claimed that he was forced to go with the hostiles to save his own life. He admitted having been at the second battle at Fort Ridgely. Otakle testified that he saw him fire his gun many times in battle. There was other testimony that he killed a woman. He admitted that he fired his gun at a woman, but he added that he did not think he killed her.

Chaskay-don (The First Born, if a son), familiarly called "Chaska": He was sentenced to hang for participating in the murder of Mr. George H. Gleason. Prior to the outbreak, he had worn white man's clothing and had been a farmer Indian. He admitted being at Lower Agency when the massacre was in progress on the first morning of the uprising. He said that he left the Lower Agency to go to Redwood with a friend, Hapa, who was his sister's husband. On the way they met Gleason, a government employee at the Upper Agency, in the company of the wife and two children of Dr. J.L. Wakefield, the agency physician. This party was traveling to Fort Ridgely, seeking safety after hearing about the uprising. He said that his friend shot

Gleason and that he intervened to save Mrs. Wakefield and her children from being killed also.

This occurred on the first morning of the outbreak, August 18. Hapa was drunk when this incident took place. After Hapa shot and killed Gleason, he might have murdered the others too, except for Chaska's intervention. At some considerable risk to himself, Chaska stopped Hapa from doing that, took the woman and two children to Chief Shakopee's camp, and protected them until they were released five weeks later at Camp Release.

During her captivity, Mrs. Wakefield lived with Chaska and his mother, who also actively participated in her protection. This favored treatment led other white captives, and other Indians as well, to believe that Chaska had taken her as his wife. In fact, she later disclosed that she even pretended to be his wife in order to better ensure her survival, but she denied that she ever was sexually involved with Chaska or that he abused her in any way.

After her release at the end of the war, Mrs. Wakefield tried to defend Chaska, especially after he was sentenced to be hanged. However, the whites perceived her as an Indian lover and not a credible witness. She did not attend the hanging when it took place as she was confident that her "protector" was not on Lincoln's list of those to be hanged, and indeed, he was not on that list.

Nevertheless, Chaska was hanged, ultimately, and later it was acknowledged that a mistake was made as there were others with the name "Chaskay-don," and this Chaska was the wrong one. The wrong man was hanged. Clearly, the Chaska that President Lincoln included in his list of those to be hanged was "No. 121 by the record." That Chaska was the 121st to be tried. The one who was supposed to be hanged had admitted to firing shots at two battles. Also, a white man testified that he had shot a woman with child and then cut her open. The Chaska who was actually hanged, however, was "No. 3 by the record." He was the 3rd person to be tried, and he was definitely not on Lincoln's list.[11]

Mrs. Wakefield believed that his execution was retribution for the affair that he was alleged to have had with her.

Baptist Campbell, a half-breed: He was convicted of murdering a man and woman. He was a son of Scott Campbell, who was later hanged at Mankato for murdering a white man long after the war was over. Baptist was less than twenty years old. He claimed to have been forced into the massacre by the Soldier's Lodge. He insisted that he did not know that he had killed anybody, although he had fired his gun a few times in two or three of the battles. Baptist was present in one of the trader's stores as the first killings took place at the Lower Agency on the first morning of the uprising.

Baptist and a brother, Hipolite Campbell, were both involved in the uprising, but they were reluctant participants. They thought at first that they would themselves be killed by the Indians because they were half-breeds. Another brother, Antoine Joseph Campbell, was a scout for the white soldiers.

Tah-ta-kay-gay (Windmaker): He was found guilty of the murder of Amos W. Huggins. Huggins had been a schoolteacher who had lived among the Wahpetons since childhood. This incident took place on the second day of the war thirty miles north of the Upper Agency, near Lac Qui Parle. Windmaker was only seventeen or eighteen years old, grandson of Sacred Walker, who took care of Mrs. Josephine Huggins and her children during their captivity. Windmaker claimed that another Indian forced him to go into the Huggins' house. At his trial he made the claim that the other Indian shot Mr. Huggins and later escaped toward Canada with Chief Little Crow as the war ended. However, a woman testified at the trial that Windmaker and the other Indian entered the house together and then there were two shots in quick succession. She said both Indians had single-barrel guns, but Windmaker said that the other Indian had a double-barrel gun and did all the shooting. Obviously, the tribunal believed the woman.

Ha-pink-pa (The Tip of the Horn): He was charged with generally participating in the uprising. He denied being involved in the major battles, saying that he stayed far off from the battles with the half-breeds. However, at his trial he was accused of the murder of Stewart B. Garvie. Two half-breeds, David Renville and Gabriel Renville, both testified that they had heard Hay-pink-pa boast of having killed Mr. Garvie with a bow and arrow.

He claimed he had lied about it in order to throw off suspicion that he was friendly with the whites. The fact is that Garvie had not been shot by an arrow at all. This was confirmed by Garvie's own statement, and he died later from a bullet wound. Hay-pink-pa was, therefore, surely innocent of the charge. He was hanged simply because he had made a boast which was a lie. Having a conscience free from guilt, he trusted the Great Spirit to save him in the other world.

Garvie was wounded on August 18, the first day of the uprising, when Indians attacked the traders' stores in the valley below the Upper Agency. One store employee was killed, but Garvie and Peter Patoile both managed to escape, each taking a different direction. Garvie made it to the brick warehouse at the Lower Agency where John Otherday had gathered most of the Agency employees and from where they all escaped the next day. Garvie was carried in a wagon because of his wounds. He died of his wounds after they reached safety in Cedar City in McLeod County.

Hypolite Auge, a half-breed: He was convicted of the murder of a white man and woman. He claimed to have been a clerk in one of the stores for a year prior to the outbreak, and that when the outbreak occurred the Indians were very suspicious of all the half-breeds. The Indians knew that many half-breeds were friendly to the whites and that to save their own scalps they might pretend to be hostile, which was often true. He admitted that he had fired at a white man in order to tell the Indians he had shot a white man and, thereby, gain their confidence. In the transcript of his trial, he is quoted as having said, "The white man was down when I fired. I fired above him. I fired as he was falling. If the white man had been standing I would have fired over him."

Na-pah-shue (One Who Does Not Flee): He actually boasted at one time that he had killed nineteen persons, but at his trial he claimed that he was forced into the war by the hostiles and did not really kill anyone.

Wa-kan-tan-ka (Great Spirit): He was charged with generally participating in the uprising. Otakle testified that he saw Wa-kan-tan-ka stab a white man and later say that he did it to avenge his brother's death. Wa-kan-tan-ka testified saying, "I did fire on whites as Godfrey [Otakle] says, but didn't kill anyone."

Toon-kan-ka-yag-e-na-jin (One Who Stands Clothed with His Grandfather): He was charged with general participation in the uprising. David Faribault testified that he was in the Big Woods when a white man was killed. He was found guilty of the murder of a white man at the Big Woods. He is quoted in the trial transcripts as saying, "I did not fire and could not fire my gun off."

Ma-kat-e-na-jin (One Who Stands on the Earth): He was convicted of committing murder near New Ulm. He was an old man. He admitted he was at the Battle of New Ulm but claimed he had not used a gun for years, and had not killed anyone. His two sons had been killed in the war.

Pa-zee-koo-tay-ma-ni (One Who Walks Prepared to Shoot): He was charged with the general charge of having participated in the uprising. He was found guilty of participating in the murder of eight white men. He said he was out with a war party against the Chippewa when the outbreak occurred, and that the war was over when he got back. He claimed that the commissioners misunderstood him when he talked about fighting the Chippewa and that he did not kill any white men. When commissioners asked him if he was in a war party and he answered "Yes," he meant against the Chippewa, and not against the whites. However, a woman testified at his trial that she heard him tell of having been in a war party that killed eight white men. In his own testimony, he said, "I didn't recollect telling anything what the witness says."

Ta-ta-hde-don (Wind Comes Home): He was charged with participating in the uprising. He admitted that he was at the battle of Beaver Creek, but he said "I was a coward and kept out of danger." He said that the men of Rice Creek were the instigators of the outbreak and that he had opposed it. He denied the charges against him. A white woman testified that he took a young white woman to his tent. Other testimony confirmed that he was at the battle of Beaver Creek.

Wa-she-choon or Toon-kan-shkan-shkan-mene-hay (Frenchman or White Man): He was found guilty of murdering LeButt's son. Wa-she-choon was a full-blooded white boy, only sixteen years old, perhaps even younger, but his white origin was not known by anyone but the Indians at the time of the hanging. He had been born at a lumber camp by the Mississippi River. His parents had both died soon thereafter. Orphaned as a baby in a lumber camp, there was nobody to care for him, so he was given to an Indian woman. She raised him as her own child among the Indians. He was in every way a Dakotah Indian except for his genetic makeup.

At his trial, and until the hanging actually took place, he denied having anything to do with the killing of white people. He did admit to having fired three shots at New Ulm. David Faribault testified, "I heard the prisoner say a few days after the outbreak [that] he shot LaBatte's son." The defendant admitted, "I fired at him but didn't hit him." As he waited to be hanged, he said that he was to die for no reason. Of all the warriors to be hanged, he was less able than anyone else to keep his composure. He cried and wept sorrowfully. The Indians who were not condemned, and who survived after the hanging, admitted that he was innocent and that his case was a particularly sad one. It has also been reported that when the name Wa-she-choon was called, as those who were to be hanged were separated from the others, there were several Indians with that name.

The boy, slightly dull-witted, responded immediately when his name was called. It has been said that he was not the one intended and was hanged by mistake. This appears to be plausible. "No. 318 by the record," was the one intended to be hanged, but perhaps this sixteen-year-old white boy was not No. 318. There were several other Indians with the name "Wa-she-choon," and the white boy who was hanged might have had a number different from 318. That number could have been any one of the others named Wa-she-choon.

A-e-cha-ga (To Grow Upon): The charges and specifications against him were the general ones of having participated in the war. However, by the testimony of Otakle, he was convicted of murdering an old man and two girls. At his trial, he made no confession, but he also did not deny the accusations of Otakle. He said, "I was there [where the old man and two girls were shot], but I don't know who shot them."

Ha-tan-inkoo (Voice That Appears Coming): He was convicted of murdering a man at Green Lake. He said that he had no gun, but that he had hit a man with a hatchet after another Indian had shot him.

Chay-ton-hoon-ka (The Parent Hawk): He was convicted of committing a murder at Beaver Creek. He admitted that he had been at the battles of Fort Ridgely and Beaver Creek and took some horses, but he denied that he killed anybody.

Chan-ka-hda (Near the Woods): The charges and specifications against him were the general ones of having participated in the war, but the phrase, "said to have captured Mary Anderson when Patoile was killed" was added. He admitted that he was present when Patoile was killed. He claimed another Indian had shot Mary Anderson in the back, wounding her severely. He said that he saved Mary Anderson from death after she had been wounded, taking her prisoner and preventing the Indian who shot her from killing her. This claim was verified by the testimony of Otakle. Chan-ka-hda thought it was unfair and much too severe that he should be hanged for a good deed.

Hda-hin-hday (To Make a Rattling Noise Suddenly): The charges and specifications against him were the general ones of having participated. He denied that he was at most of the battles, saying that he was "at home with a belly-ache." He admitted he was at the battle of Wood Lake but said that the charge against him was entirely false as he "did not fire a gun." However, at his trial, a woman testified that she had heard that he was the man who killed the child of Mrs. Adams. Another woman testified that Mrs. Adams had pointed him out as the one who killed her child. Apparently, all of this was enough to get him hanged.

O-ya-tay-a-koo (The Coming People): He was convicted of murdering Patoile by striking him with his hatchet after he had been shot. He admitted that he was with the party that killed Patoile, but denied the charge of striking him with his hatchet.

May-hoo-way-wa (He Comes for Me): Charged with the general participation in the uprising, he was convicted of committing murder at the Traveler's Home on the basis of Otakle's testimony. He admitted to having participated in one of the raids toward the Big Woods. He denied that he had actually killed anyone himself, but was himself wounded during the war when a white man shot him with a pistol.

Wa-kin-yan-na (Little Thunder): He was charged with the general participation in the uprising, but he was found guilty of participating in the murder of an old man, two girls, and two boys near the Traveler's Home. Otakle testified that he heard Little Thunder say that he killed the two boys with his war lance. The defendant then said, "I might have done it, but it was not with my lance . . ."

The Indians generally were resigned to their fate. Few of them gave much thought to the possibility of escape. Some protested their sentence to be hanged, proclaiming their innocence, but most just said nothing about it in the traditional stoic Indian fashion.

They watched from the small windows of their prison as the scaffold was being constructed. They could see that preparations were being made to hang a large group simultaneously. The prospect of being hanged in a group as opposed to being hanged one by one was unexpectedly comforting—they would not be dying alone as they would if hanged one by one. They made plans for the event, deciding what their death song would be and making certain that everyone knew all the words. Not one of them should show any fear at any time.

The noise of the construction was more than somewhat bothersome. They tried to ignore it but found that the pounding, sawing, and the cheer-ful chatter of the workmen and soldiers in the nearby construction area was quite inescapably annoying.

Cut Nose watched all the activity more closely than the others. It was as if he wanted to know every detail of the preparations. Secretly, he was looking for some fault in them, some mistake in the construction that might give him a chance to change his fate.

The other condemned men were openly displeased with Cut Nose. After all, as the leader of the Soldier's Lodge, he was at least partially respon-sible for getting them into this fix.

"What are you looking at, you fool," one of them said to him as Cut Nose stared out the window. "You'll soon be dangling by your neck up there with the rest of us."

"Don't be too sure about that," said Cut Nose.

He had been watching as the workmen had fashioned the nooses and attached them to the scaffold. Some of the ropes were frayed and damaged. He noticed one in particular that looked as if it would break easily if it were jerked hard. It was the first one to the left of the stairway leading to the platform of the scaffold. He decided that this should be his rope, and he began to develop a strategy for making sure that this would be his place.

At the next daily rehearsal of the death song which would be sung at the hanging, Cut Nose proposed that as leader of the Soldier's Lodge he should lead the procession to the execution. "It should be my responsibility to go first," he said.

Someone argued that the spiritual leader among them should go first. However, most agreed with Cut Nose, that he should go first. Some held that opinion because they agreed that the leader of the Soldier's Lodge should go first, others because they were mad at Cut Nose and wanted to hang him themselves. In the end, Cut Nose won the position.

Two days before the scheduled execution day, each prisoner was allowed to visit with members of his family. Conversations were relatively pleasant and newsy instead of what might be expected under such somber circumstances. Family members told of the mass move to Fort Snelling and the accommodations there. They also told of the abuses to which they had been subjected enroute to the fort, including the killing of the baby at Henderson. But there was a lot of small talk, too, like, "How are the children?" "Do you get enough to eat?" "Did you remember to take my buffalo robe and my pipe?"

The next day, the day before the hanging was to take place, there was more visiting, and the prisoners had an opportunity to say their good-byes. The conversations on this day were much sadder. There was much crying by the relatives. The prisoners told the relatives of their preparations for dying and of their death song and their rehearsals. The prisoners themselves were sad but most did not weep. They were mostly quite resolute in their attitude. A few were angry, believing that it was wrong for them to be executed. They complained about the injustice of what was about to happen, but they did not cry.

As they departed, many of the visitors asked about taking the remains of their loved one for burial and were told that this would not be allowed. They were told that the Army would bury the bodies in a secret place. This caused more sobbing. Also, the relatives would not be allowed to attend the execution but instead would be required to return to Fort Snelling immediately under escort. The civilian population had a mind to hang all the Indians and might not stop with just forty if the relatives were still around. Nevertheless, some relatives, at great risk to their own safety, were among the crowd of spectators at the time of the hanging.

Many of the condemned were baptized as Christians before the execution. It is of interest that most were baptized Catholic despite the fact that the protestant minister had spent many more years serving them. The split was impressive—thirty-three Catholics to three Protestants—surprising even to the priest who did all this baptizing. The reason for the choice that the Indians made, however, was discovered to be equally surprising. It was learned that they admired the priest's long black robe (cassock) and they thought that if they were to be baptized Catholic they might be given a robe like that.

An hour before the appointed time for the hanging to take place, last minute preparations were completed. The sentence of Round Wind was commuted. He would not be hanged and was separated from the others, leaving just thirty-eight to be hanged. All of these were fitted with "caps" which were, in actuality, unbleached muslin bags that would cover their faces when they were hanged, but until the noose was actually put around their necks, the bags were rolled up so that they could see and breathe more easily. The Indians objected to these bags, thinking that they were humiliating, but none were allowed to refuse to wear them. The shackles on their legs were removed. Then they all had their elbows shackled behind them and their hands bound in front, about six inches apart at the wrists.

The white clergymen who were present prayed for them in Dakotah and spoke to them in English, their words translated by Baptist Campbell, one of the half-breeds waiting to be hanged. At the appointed time, all was in readiness.

All the thirty-eight were dressed in fine, beaded buckskins except for the three half-breeds who were dressed in white men's clothing. The Indians marched from their common cell right on cue, singing their death song even as they climbed the steps to the platform. Cut Nose went first, as he had planned, walking to the right at the top of the steps and all the way around the platform to end up at exactly the first spot to the left of the steps, the place with the frayed rope.

There were approximately fourteen hundred soldiers in formation around the scaffold. Thousands of civilian spectators from as far as fifty miles away were present to witness the hanging. Every rooftop and vantage point was crowded with spectators. They watched as soldiers unrolled the cap-bag over the head and face of each Indian and fixed the noose snuggly around the neck of each one. The crowd became quiet as a drum started to sound the signal to cut the cable supporting the scaffold. The stabilizing props under the platform were knocked away and the platform became shaky. The Indians continued their death song, some holding hands with their neighbor, straining against the shackles and the noose to do so. Then, on the third beat of the drum, a man who had lost several of his family during the massacres swung an axe to cut the main support cable. In his eagerness, he failed to sever it with the first swing, but the job was done with the second. The main support cable was cut and the platform dropped with a crash. The crowd was silent at first, but then roared as the Indians' death song stopped and the thirty-eight lives ended.

Cut Nose put his plan into action just as the supporting platform was falling away. He braced himself and fell as hard as he could against the rope, believing that there was a good chance it would break, frayed as it was. And he was right—the rope broke, and he fell to the platform on the ground in a heap.[12]

Unfortunately for Cut Nose, however, the great force it took to break the rope was enough to break his neck, too. In the moments of consciousness remaining for him, he tried to escape, but all he could do was convulsively kick and roll over, and roll over he did, over and over again, moving slowly toward the river. And then the darkness came.

90

Two soldiers ran up to him as he rolled downhill toward the river. Standing over Cut Nose, one of the soldiers said, excitedly, "This guy is still moving, but he's dead. His neck looks like it's broke. Jesus! Look at him twitch!"

"String that bastard back up there until he's good and dead! That's Cut Nose," said a sergeant. "By God, I should have expected it. That rotten cow plop is too damn mean to die with just one hanging."

Two soldiers grabbed the loose end of the broken rope still around his neck and dragged Cut Nose unceremoniously by the neck back to the spot where he landed on the platform when he fell. While the soldiers dragged Cut Nose across the ground he continued to twitch a little, most likely reflexively, but it looked like he was complaining a little about the rough treatment he was receiving. Soon his body laid limp on the collapsed platform as the soldiers hastily tied a length of new rope to the broken one still around his neck. They threw the new rope over the beam from which he had fallen. Then the soldiers hoisted Cut Nose up to the same level as the others, hanging him again, and tied the rope off on the center post of the scaffold. By now, the other Indians were just gently swinging. There was no more singing, no more kicking, no more complaints, no more struggle among any of the thirty-eight Indians hanging there. And Cut Nose, individually, had the attention of the entire large crowd of thousands of spectators and soldiers.

In all the commotion as he rolled toward the river, Cut Nose's "cap" had come off. Nobody had bothered to put it back on. What now presented itself was a most bizarre and grotesque spectacle. Cut Nose was now literally facing the crowds below, his eyes wide open, slightly bulging from their sockets, and his tongue protruding from his mouth. His face appeared to have a very angry and intense expression as he slowly rotated around and around on his rope to look down in turn at every one of the thousands of faces staring back at him. It was as though in death he was making one last statement in the only way he could. The statement that he was making hushed the crowd.

Indian people believe that the manner in which a person dies is as important as the way one lives. It is the final opportunity to display bravery, the highest value of the Dakotahs. The thirty-eight died bravely, and, in doing so, they deprived the white people of at least some of the satisfaction that they might otherwise have obtained. There was no justice in these hangings. Instead, they added only one more horrible disgrace to the tragedies of the war.

Within minutes the crowd began to quietly disburse.

Ten minutes after the platform dropped, two local doctors began to examine each of the Indians to determine that all were dead. One was still alive after hanging for all that time. The rope on this one was adjusted so that the noose would strangle him more effectively while the doctors went about examining the rest of those still hanging. After twenty minutes, all were declared dead and were then cut down and loaded into four waiting wagons to be transported to the burial site, a single trench that had been excavated on the river bottom some distance upstream from the hanging site. The grave was only four feet deep, thirty feet long and twelve feet wide, but it was large enough to accommodate all thirty-eight bodies. They were laid out in pairs, feet-to-feet, in a single layer. Then the dirt was thrown right in their faces. They were not covered with anything at all except with the dirt that had been taken from the hole. There was a mound of sandy dirt over the grave when the shoveling was done. A squad of soldiers remained at the grave until nightfall to guard against any possible looting. Then a single guard remained to guard the grave through the night. Since the grave was secretly located, nobody expected any trouble.

Chapter Nine

෨ ◆ ಌ

The Incredible Grave Robbery

A S IF THE SIMULTANEOUS HANGING of thirty-eight human beings was not sufficiently astounding, what happened later that night was absolutely dumfounding. Few people had given much thought to what would happen to the bodies after the hanging. The relatives were saddened and extremely displeased that they were not allowed to take the bodies with them for burial in a dignified manner according to Indian custom. They were not told what the plans were for the disposal of the bodies, only that they could not have them.

The shallow mass grave where the bodies were buried was in a sand bar near the river. This site would flood almost every spring, and it might have been selected for that very reason. In the spring the bodies might be washed away so that the grave, bodies and all, might just disappear and nevermore cause anybody any concern. As it turned out, the bodies disappeared all right, but much sooner than expected.

Some local doctors conspired to take the bodies from the grave during the night, freeze them, and sell them for use as cadavers. Each body was worth more than a month's pay for a soldier. It was late in December and temperatures were very cold. Frozen, the bodies would be preserved while they were shipped as far as Chicago. Then they could be thawed out and used for medical study. There is some irony in the fact that while alive, these Indians were considered by many to be sub-human, but now, in death, they were deemed to be acceptable for use as human cadavers.

With two wagons, each with a team of horses, the doctors and other people helping them were coming to get the bodies. They approached the gravesite cautiously and were stopped by the lone soldier guarding the site. He had been watching as they approached. He was quite surprised to see anyone in that area, and a little frightened, as might be imagined. By now it was pitch dark and guarding a fresh grave with thirty-eight fresh bodies on a dark night was not the best duty a soldier could get.

"Halt!" he ordered when the approaching party was near enough.

"It's okay. It's me, Captain Mayo. You know me, don't you?"

"Yes, sir. Come on ahead then," replied the soldier who was greatly relieved to hear a familiar voice. He knew Captain Mayo, all right. In fact, he knew him as somewhat of a rascal who would do most anything for a buck. It was well known that he did physical examinations on the young men being drafted for service in the Army, and there were stories that for a few dollars passed under the table he might be convinced to find the inductee physically unfit for service.[13]

Approaching the guard alone, Captain Mayo removed a glove to return the guard's salute and then, unexpectedly, to shake the guard's hand in a friendly way, saying, "What's your name, soldier?"

"I'm Private Olson, sir, Tenth Minnesota, Infantry."

"Looks like you drew the short straw for this duty, Private Olson. You're here by yourself, aren't you? How would you like to have some company?"

"I would like some company for sure, sir, but I don't think you came here to keep me company. What are you doing here?" Olson was an intelligent lad and knew that something was fishy.

"I'm going to let you in on something. We're here to get all these Indian bodies, and we need your cooperation. We'll make it worth your while, and all you have to do is keep your mouth shut. Don't tell anybody about this."

"I don't know, sir." The guard was skeptical. "I have to clear this with my commanding officer."

"Well, that would be the best thing, but you can't do that, Private Olson. We can't wait at all, not even until tomorrow. If we get them out of the ground now, they'll freeze right away and stay fresh. But if we leave them in that grave, even overnight, they'll start to get ripe by morning."

The others were now standing by and entered into the efforts to persuade Private Olson. "We need 'em for cadavers. They're gonna be used for medical science. They gotta be fresh. At least, they can't be rotten. If we wait 'til tomorrow, they'll heat up."

"They could generate enough heat to warm the ground if the ground is cold. But if we wait the top few inches of the ground will freeze from this cold, and then it will be just as hard to dig 'em out as it was to dig this damn hole in the first place." They all knew how difficult it is to dig through frozen earth in Minnesota in the winter, and some of them had helped to dig that grave.

"Especially the way they're piled in there together. They're keepin' each other warm, and the ground is keepin' 'em warm too. I'll bet it's still plenty warm under the ground." With the setting of the sun the temperature had dropped rapidly, but the earth covering the bodies would provide some insulation from the cold. The temperature during the night at this time of the year would often drop to well below zero.

The men began to talk as if the deal with the guard had already been made. "When we get 'em out, we have to spread 'em out so they'll cool off good 'n proper. We really ought to hang 'em up again off the ground—strip 'em naked—that'd be the best way to freeze 'em."

"Nah, we don't have to do all that. But we do have to get them out of the ground to freeze 'em.[14] That's enough work for one night. We split 'em up, load 'em on the wagons so they're not all piled up and keepin' each other warm, and they'll freeze. I've done it before with a lot of critters—and with a few dead people, too."

"Once they're frozen clear through, we can ship 'em anywhere. Left outside they'll stay frozen 'til March for sure. Cover 'em up with some straw and canvas so the sun can't get at 'em and they'll stay frozen for months, clear into April."

"We'll give you ten dollars just to keep quiet," said Dr. Mayo. "We'll do all the work. When you get relieved in the morning you just act like nothing happened and nobody will be the wiser. What do you say?"

Ten dollars was a lot of money to Private Olson, and, after all, a captain was making the offer. And this night was shaping up to be a lot better than he had anticipated. So, without much hesitation, Private Olson agreed.

"Whatever you say, sir."

The earth piled up over the bodies was still loose as the men began to shovel it away. The first part was easy—just a matter of scooping the dirt away. But as they approached the level where they would find the bodies they were more careful, not wanting to damage any of the bodies with their shovels. Piled in there as the bodies were, the ground above the bodies became springy when the diggers got close. They could then reach into the loose dirt and grab a limb or clothing and pull the top bodies out. The remaining dirt didn't matter as it just seemed to filter down between the remaining bodies. It didn't take long to get all thirty-eight out. Most of the bodies were rigid with rigor mortis, but a few were still limp.

Soon, both wagons were loaded, and the hole was back-filled. Private Olson had not wanted to have anything to do with the bodies, but in order to get the job done and make the area look like nothing had happened, he pitched in to help fill the hole. There had been a mound of dirt over the grave when the bodies were still in it, but now there was just about enough dirt to fill the hole with the bodies missing from it. In fact, with a considerable amount of the original dirt scattered around the hole, not quite enough dirt could be gathered to fill up the trench again, and a slight depression remained in the ground. Still, the hole would be hard to find after a snowfall if one didn't know exactly where it was to begin with. It was intended that the gravesite would be kept a secret from most folks. And even now snow was falling quite heavily.

There was no road to the gravesite, but there was a rough trail that had been left by the wagons that brought the thirty-eight bodies to the riverbank. Captain Mayo had come down that trail with his wagons, too, and now was following that trail up the hill again with all the bodies loaded on the wagons. In a couple of spots the way up the hill from the riverside was extremely rough. One of the bodies fell off a wagon without even being noticed by the driver in the haste to depart the area and the urgency to get to a higher level of ground. When the body fell off the end of the wagon it rolled to the side of the trail. The second wagon nearly ran over it, but in the darkness the second wagon's driver didn't see the body and continued on without stopping.

It was hours later, in the dim light of dawn that the body was discovered by a squad of soldiers on their way to relieve Private Olson at the gravesite. When it was first spotted, the soldiers thought it was an Indian lying in ambush, and they shot it. These were fresh green troops, and all four of them shot it, not just once, but twice. By then they were pretty sure that the Indian was dead, but as they approached the body one of them shot it again to be certain.

"Good God, we must have killed him right off because he didn't bleed at all," one of them said.

"What the hell did you shoot him again for?" one remarked with poorly assumed righteousness. "He was already dead. Hell, I can see at least two head shots besides yours. His head's practically blowed off."

"Where the hell did he come from?" said another.

"He must have come from over there," said another, looking upstream, "and by God, there's another one!"

They had all lifted their rifles to take aim before they saw that it was Private Olson approaching.

"Don't shoot," he yelled, crouching a bit just in case. "I heard the shooting. What's happening?"

"This damn Indian was creeping up on us and we shot him," the one that had shot him last reported with pride.

"Damn," said Private Olson as he looked at the dead Indian. "You sure did!"

"Have you seen any more Indians?" asked one of the soldiers.

"No!" Private Olson snapped back perhaps a little too quickly. Now Private Olson was worried. He figured this was almost surely one of the thirty-eight hanged men and that the body had fallen off a wagon because this Indian wasn't dressed for the weather. "You say he was creepin' up on ya?" he asked with poorly suppressed skepticism.

"Well, yeah. We spotted him there waitin' for us as we come to relieve you. I guess we all shot him. You see any more Indians during the night?"

"Not a one," Olson lied again. "Nothing happened at all."

"Well, I guess this one was just at the wrong place at the wrong time," said one of the soldiers who had been examining the body. "He ain't even armed."

"That right? Maybe he was one of the thirty-eight hanged, and he fell off the wagon on the way to the grave," Private Olson ventured with some risk. "What do you think of that?"

"Hell, no," said the one who shot him last. "He was sneakin' up on us. We all saw him. We all shot him. Didn't we?" he said as he looked at the others for support. They all looked at each other and agreed.

"Well, look at him. He's got to be one of the ones that got hung. He ain't dressed for this weather, he's unarmed, he's all by himself—what kind of Indian is goin' to come down here all by himself with no weapons and attack the four of you in the middle of the night?"

"Well, those are some pretty good points you got there," said one of the four, "but how are we gonna explain that we shot up a redskin that was already dead? We'd look pretty stupid if we did that."

"Just say you knew he was dead when you found him so you figured it wouldn't hurt him if you had a little fun and used him for target practice."

Once again, the four looked at each other in agreement over this face-saving idea. Instead of looking dumb, this story would make them look like tough, seasoned, Indian fighters, they thought. To give their story more credibility, they actually tied the body upright to a tree and shot it a few more times.[15] As they were doing this, more soldiers showed up on the scene. The officer among them was very opposed to what was happening and ordered them to stop shooting.

With that matter settled, they went on with their business. Olson pointed out the way to the gravesite and headed back for camp to report the shooting and take his well-earned rest. The others headed for the gravesite, but they were not able to find it. They went in the general direction indicated by Private Olson, and they stayed on what they thought was the trail, but the snow had continued to fall quite heavily and by now there were several inches of snow on the ground. They couldn't find anything that looked like a burial mound. It didn't make much difference, they figured. There were no more Indians around, and nobody was coming around looking for souvenirs. It is an absolute fact that to this day nobody has ever found that exact gravesite again.

ⅆ ◆ ⅇ

WHEN THE WAGONS FULL OF BODIES cleared the woods, it was still hours before daybreak. At that time of the night nobody was in sight, and they drove the wagons right through Mankato with the bodies without being observed. They made a bee line for a farm on the way to St Peter. They had arranged to use the barn for laying out the bodies for freezing. It was plenty cold enough to freeze the bodies solid in no time at all. Once inside the barn, the bodies could be laid out with plenty of space between them. Both ends of the barn would be opened up to allow the icy wind to blow through. The bodies would be arranged so as to have as much exposure to the cold wind as possible. The wind would whisk away any body heat left in them. The purpose of all this was to freeze all the bodies solid as quickly as possible in order to preserve them, so they could be shipped even as far as Chicago, several hundred miles away, to be sold for medical use as cadavers.

The wagons arrived at the barn before daybreak, and the men unloaded the bodies and laid them out in the open loft in less than an hour. The loft was empty except for all the bodies laid out neatly in two rows stretching from one end of the forty-foot barn to the other. When the work was done the men counted the bodies and found that there were only thirty-seven. Captain Mayo counted again and then recounted a third time. There were definitely nineteen bodies in one row and only eighteen in the other.

There was initially some concern that one of the bodies might have fallen off one of the wagons, but after some discussion they came to the conclusion that one must have been left in the bottom of the hole at the gravesite. In their haste, and in the dark, that could have happened easily, they reasoned, although they had counted thirty-eight bodies at the gravesite. After some argument, they finally decided that they must have miscounted at the gravesite. One body at the bottom of that grave wouldn't make much difference to anyone, they thought. One body was not much revenue lost. It didn't matter.[17]

Now they could relax because only a few trusted people knew where they were. Even with the bodies as much exposed to the cold as they were in the opened up barn, it was not likely that anyone passing on the closest road would spot them. Dr. Mayo looked at the bodies carefully and recognized Cut Nose and a few others. He selected these to take with him when he left to go to his home in LeSueur, which was at least a day's trip with his wagon.

"Help me load a few of these bucks on my wagon," he said to one of the men. "I'm taking my share with me right now. But remember, I get some of the money we get for these others, too."

He went down one line of bodies and picked out two. Then he started back up the other line and picked out another, and then he spotted Cut Nose and said, "I want this one especially. He once tried to take my horse from me." Two of the men began loading the bodies he wanted. Though all of the bodies were cold and stiff with rigor mortis, there was still some flexibility in them. They had not yet frozen completely solid. Dr. Mayo thought that they would continue to cool and freeze even as he traveled with them.

When the four bodies that he had selected were loaded on the back of his buckboard and covered with a canvas, the little doctor hitched up his horse and started out for St Peter. By now, it was nearly mid-morning and the daylight seemed quite bright despite the heavy cloud cover, which was usual for this time of the year. There were few people on the trail, as most folks didn't travel much this time of the year. If he did meet someone they wouldn't be at all surprised that he had a load in his buckboard because, after all, everyone knew he was in the freight business. Covered with canvas as they were, the bodies could be sacks of flour as far as anyone could tell, and no one would ask questions. The way he calculated it, he would have no trouble at all getting these bodies moved with no one being the wiser.

The doctor's efforts to be discreet in the theft of the bodies is interesting in the context of the high probability that nobody would care or object to what he was doing if they knew full well that he was hauling off the bodies of hanged Indians. It may be that he knew, at some level of consciousness, that this whole business was morally wrong and reprehensible, so he felt that it would be best to hide them. It is likely that he thought that this caper would reflect badly on him if he were to be found out. No doubt he had some feelings of culpability associated with it. Nevertheless, he was an opportunist who would not let pass this excellent chance to make a few extra dollars.

He had made a private agreement with a group of men from New Ulm to sell three of the bodies to them for thirty dollars. They had paid him half when the agreement was made, and he would get the other half when the bodies were obtained. These men were not medical men and the captain had no idea what they were going to do with the bodies, but he didn't care much either. He had made arrangements for them to pick up the bodies at a St. Peter building owned by a close friend.

When he arrived at St Peter it was mid-afternoon, but already it was starting to get dark. He hadn't slept for two days. After dark, with the help of his friend, the three bodies were carried discreetly to the roof of the building where they would remain until they were claimed by the men from New Ulm who purchased them. By now, the little doctor was exhausted. The trip to LeSueur would take most of another day. He decided to spend the night in St Peter where his friend gave him a good hot supper and a warm bed for a good night's sleep. The one body that remained on the buckboard was that of Cut Nose. The night was very cold, well below zero degrees Fahrenheit, and by morning all the bodies would be frozen solid. Few people ventured out on a night like this and the little doctor was not worried that someone might discover what was under the canvas on his buckboard.

Chapter Ten

❧ ◆ ❧

The Posthumous Career of Cut Nose

OCTOR MAYO ARRIVED AT HIS HOME in LeSueur with the body of Cut Nose the next day. He put the body in the woodshed and covered it with canvas to lie in state until he was ready to deal with it. Eventually he would bring it into the house to thaw it out, call a meeting of all the local medical people, and dissect it for the benefit of their education. After that, the bones of Cut Nose, cleaned of every speck of flesh and dried thoroughly, would repose in a large cast-iron rendering kettle in his office. He would use them for reference and for instruction of his patients, helping them to understand the nature of their injuries or problems.[18]

While living in Le Sueur, Doctor Mayo's practice was either in his own home or out in the fields or in the homes of the people who lived in the area within ten or fifteen miles which, round trip, was nearly a day's travel. One of his boys, Will, was born in the doctor's little house in LeSueur, but he was too young to have very much real appreciation for his father's work activities while they lived there. The family moved to Rochester by the time Will was four years old. Still, the house in LeSueur was so small that, even as a toddler, Will could not have escaped being involved, to some extent, with his father's activities. In the absence of many toys to get his attention, it is easy to imagine that Will might have been quite fascinated with the big cast-iron kettle full of human bones in his dad's office.

These were the bones of Cut Nose, all jumbled up, clean and white, disconnected, mixed together in no particular order, kept as reference material for Doctor W.W. to use as he explained things to his patients. If someone came in with a broken leg, for example, the doctor would fish out the leg bone corresponding to the broken one and use it as a visual aid as he explained to his patient exactly where the break was, what needed to be done to fix it, why a splint or cast was necessary, and so on. These bones were a marvelous help when it came to explaining things to patients. Most of the patients had some experience with butchering various kinds of animals, and it was easy for them to visualize and understand a lot of what the doctor was talking about. They were usually more agreeable when they understood what was required.

For Will Mayo, at four years of age, these bones were something else. They were a puzzle, like a jigsaw puzzle. It started with the skull. The top part of the skull was very easy to recognize as such, and the jawbone obviously belonged with it, the lower teeth so neatly opposed to the uppers. The rest of the puzzle was not so very easy, however, and the skeleton provided hours of effort to assemble completely. Many of the bones required very careful study and comparison before they could be correctly placed in the skeleton. Some bones were very similar to others and some didn't seem to have an obvious place in the scheme of things at all. Considerations of shape and size helped to get started, but some very detailed study was necessary to discriminate right from left in some of the small bones, especially, and there were also very few differences between some of the vertebrae in the spinal column.

Will would string the vertebrae together on a piece of rope and use pieces of string to tie the other bones in place. His dad would correct his mistakes and explain to him the reason for each bone being in a certain place, why it was out of place elsewhere. In order to talk about the bones more easily, W.W. provided the technical names for each of them. Before long, they all had a proper name. The method of tying things together was improved to permit the bones to be moved in opposition to each other the way they were when Cut Nose was alive. Ultimately, the skeleton was very well articulated.

Later on, when Charlie was born and old enough, Will took pride and pleasure in teaching Charlie all about these bones. It is well documented as historical fact, and acknowledged in Charles Mayo's autobiography, that the famous Mayo brothers learned all about bones from playing with the skeleton of Cut Nose. These two boys both became doctors and were destined to become two of the most famous doctors in the world, founders of the world-renowned Mayo Clinic in Rochester, Minnesota.

For many years after the Mayo Clinic was established, the fully articulated skeleton of Cut Nose was displayed in the lobby of the Clinic. Then it was moved to the museum where hundreds of visitors weekly could not only view it, but also touch it. Visitors could actually take Cut Nose's hand and shake it in a friendly gesture. So many visitors did so that the hands had to be replaced, according to the museum curator.

The curator told me, just before his retirement, that the skeleton displayed had been in the museum for at least fifty years. He could not say where the skeleton came from. He knew about the Cut Nose skeleton, but he was not certain that this skeleton was that of Cut Nose. Together, he and I took the skeleton down from its display to examine it closely. We looked at every bone. There were no clearinghouse marks or any other marks of any kind on any of the bones which might identify its source. There was no dentistry in any of the teeth. The molars were worn flat. Two teeth were missing, an eyetooth of the left uppers and a canine of the right lowers. There was damage to one of the cervical vertebrae. All of these findings were consistent with the possibility that the skeleton was, indeed, that of Cut Nose.

I asked my own dentist about the flat molars I had observed. He told me that flat molars might be the result of a lifetime of chewing gritty food cooked over an open fire. Ash is very abrasive, he explained.

The complete lack of dentistry is an indication that the skeleton was very old. The missing teeth in front were likely the result of trauma because the rest of the teeth were intact and healthy looking except for the wear. Cut Nose was a fighter and could have had those front teeth knocked out.

I corresponded with the archivist at Mayo Clinic with an exchange of several letters, but it is clear now that the clinic was not willing to own up to having any part of the skeleton of Cut Nose in its possession. It is likely that the clinic denied it because of the modern-day political incorrectness of admitting to having such material in its possession. I exchanged several letters with the clinic archivist, and there are several letters from him in my file, all completely denying possessing any of the bones of Cut Nose. My first letter to the archivist and my last letter to him are reproduced below:

May 3, 1990

Director, Mayo Historical Unit
Mayo Clinic
Rochester, MN., 55095

Dear Mr. _____,

After talking on the phone with you today I was left with the impression that you know all about Cut Nose and that it is your belief that the Cut Nose skeleton no longer exists. I am writing to inquire whether you can state with certainty that the skeleton hanging in the Education Center [located in the Damon Parking Ramp Building] is not that of one of the thirty-eight Indians who were hanged in Mankato on Dec. 26, 1864. I Have a strong suspicion that the skeleton you have hanging there is that of Cut Nose.

There is much evidence to support my suspicion. There are historical reports that the father of the Mayo brothers, Dr. W.W. Mayo took the body of Cut Nose from the mass grave where the Indians were placed after they were hanged. After dissecting the body for the benefit of the local medical community, he articulated the bones and had that skeleton hanging in his office for many years. Dr. C.W. Mayo acknowledged as much in his autobiography.

I have examined the skeleton in question quite carefully. Certain observations are consistent with the hypothesis that this skeleton could be the remains of Cut Nose. There are no "clearing house marks" on any of the bones as determined by close inspection by myself and the curator [name omitted], in about 1984. There is no dental work in any of the teeth. The two teeth missing appear to have been lost due to trauma as evidenced by the broken sockets. The molars are worn flat as is typical among the Indians, who ate many foods raw and who cooked over open fires, often getting ash (an abrasive) in their food. Cut Nose was described as a fighter, a rough and tough guy who probably did get a couple of teeth knocked out during his lifetime. Lastly, I can personally recall seeing a protograph of a skeleton in the lobby of the Mayo Clinic many years ago which was captioned "Cut Nose," this protograph long since having been removed. Would that photo still be in your archives?

[Name omitted] informed me that the skeleton in question has been in the possession of the Clinic for more than fifty years, although he was unable to say with certainty that it is or is not that of Cut Nose. He said that many people have inquired about it, including some Indians occasionally. I am interested in determining once and for all whether this skeleton is that of Cut Nose, or if the skeleton of Cut Nose is still in the possession of the Mayo family or the Clinic.

You may already know that each Summer, in the "Land of Memories" Park in Mankato, there is an Indian Pow Wow held to commemorate and honor the 38 Indians who were hanged there in 1864. While attending that Pow Wow each Summer I am bothered by the nagging feeling that one of these honored dead might still be hanging.

If there is any way that modern technology could help to identify that skeleton, I would think that the Mayo Clinic would have that technology at its disposal. I suggest that the Clinic should use it to resolve the question I have posed once and for all. Furthermore, in the event that the skeleton does turn out to be that of Cut Nose, or if the Mayo family has possession of the remains of Cut Nose, then it would be a grand gesture of reconciliation indeed for the Clinic or the Mayo family to return those relics to the appropriate Indian authorities for proper burial.

Sincerely yours,
/S/
Loren D. Boutin, Ph.D.

When the foregoing letter was written I had not been involved with the powwow or the Indians or the Mdewakanton Association very long and was still quite naïve about many things. I spelled powwow as "Pow Wow," for example. I even stated the wrong year for the hanging. Despite my naivete, however, the archivist for Mayo Clinic responded to my letter as follows:

Mayo Foundation
Rochester, Minnesota 55901
Telephone 507 282-2511

March 13, 1991

Archives

Loren D. Boutin, Ph.D.
513 North Minnesota Avenue
St Peter, MN 56082

Dear Dr. Boutin,

I have carefully reviewed, with several Clinic colleagues, the question that you have posed concerning a Mayo skeleton. Unfortunately, we have no evidence to substantiate your thoughts about it being that of an historic Indian. The skeleton was purchased in recent times for use in educational programs at Mayo. It is not an historic artifact.

The previously mentioned materials were available, some 23 years ago, about the time that the Indians obtained Little Crow's remains from the Minnesota Historical Society and then buried them near Faribault. At that time, an extensive effort was made at Mayo to examine all older skeletal materials to see if they could possibly be Indian in origin and date back to the 1862 period. None could be so identified, but those that might be suspect were shown to the Indians, who expressed no interest.

Interestingly, the Mayo story about Cut Nose varies among the members of the Mayo family. Dr. Charlie referred to a kettle in which the bones were kept. If true, this could imply that only a minimal number of bones from Cut Nose's body were available. Given the circumstances in that period, how long such remains would survive is questionable.

At any rate, the skeleton you have identified has no connections with the era, and I am unable to offer anything concrete as to what did happen to Cut Nose or any of his companions. I do hope that this helps. Thanks for the interest.

Sincerely yours,
/S/

———————————
Mayo Historical Unit

For me, Mr. [name omitted]'s response was quite unsatisfactory. From what he wrote, it is obvious that he had no knowledge about the kind of "kettle" in which the bones were stored. It was a big cast-iron rendering kettle, sufficiently ample in size to accommodate the entire skeleton of Cut Nose with room to spare. It took me awhile to digest that letter and then get back to him, but what follows is the last of my communications with him:

Feb. 15, 1993

Mayo Historical Unit
Mayo Foundation
Rochester, MN 5590

Dear Mr. _____,

It was a long time ago, but I hope you might recall some previous correspondence that we have had about a skeleton that was hanging in the Mayo Education Center which I had thought might be the remains of Cut Nose, one of the 38 Indians who were hanged in Mankato in 1862. In your last letter to me (dated March 13, 1991), you told me of having consulted with some colleagues at Mayo and you told me your reasons for thinking that the skeleton was not that of Cut Nose or any other historic Indian.

While I appreciate the efforts that you have apparently made to assure me that this particular skeleton, the one which was hanging in the Education Center, is not that of an historic Indian, I must say that I am nevertheless disappointed in that you provided no conclusive evidence to support your side of the question. Your consultation with colleagues and the assertion that the skeleton "was purchased in recent times" is not persuasive.

Your description of efforts made 25 years ago to identify any skeletal material at Mayo as being Indian in origin is interesting, but also not persuasive. At about that time, I can personally recall seeing in the lobby of the Clinic a picture of an articulated skeleton with the caption, "Cut Nose." I have been told by someone at the Clinic that this picture is probably filed somewhere in your archives. Can you find that?

If, as you say, the Indians were not interested in skeletal remains twenty-five years ago, I can assure you that they are now. As a member of the Mdewakanton Club in Mankato, which each fall sponsors the annual powwow to honor the 38 Indians who were hanged in 1862, I am personally interested.

If it is true that you are, as you said, "unable to offer anything concrete as to what did happen to Cut Nose or any of his companions," then can you give me any kind of lead as to where I might search next? Can someone in the Mayo family help? Surely there must be some record of what happened to the remains of this historic Indian.

Sincerely yours,

Loren D. Boutin, Ph.D.

This letter yielded no response, and the archivist retired shortly thereafter.

There was an occasion after that when I had opportunity to accompany the official Sacred Pipe Carrier for the Dakotah Nation, Arvol Lookinghorse, to the site where the hanging of the thirty-eight took place. As I told him about the hanging and what happened to the remains of those hanged, I mentioned my unsuccessful efforts to retrieve the remains of Cut Nose.

The woman with him said, "If anyone can get the clinic to give them up, he can." So, in May of 1993, I sent a package of all my correspondence with Mayo Clinic to Mr. Lookinghorse. I did not hear anything from him, but about six months later the clinic did submit two skulls to Hamline University for forensic analysis and the determination as to whether either could be identified as that of Cut Nose. I found that very interesting, because with me the clinic spokesman had denied any knowledge whatsoever regarding the location of any remains of Cut Nose. One of the skulls was found to have a high probability of being that of Cut Nose. This skull was ceremoniously buried at the Lower Sioux Reservation on May 19, 1998. The Indians at his burial ranked Cut Nose as a chief. The eulogy was given by the spiritual leader at the burial ceremony who was Ed Red Owl, a direct descendant of Cut Nose.

Two years later, as a result of the Native American Graves Protection and Repatriation Act, an inventory of items in the Public Museum of Grand Rapids, Michigan, identified a piece of Cut Nose's skin, tanned and tattooed for identification. This piece of skin was fairly large, about four inches by five inches in dimension. Nobody seems to know how this curious artifact made its way to Michigan. It, too, was returned to the Lower Sioux Reservation near Morton, Minnesota, where the newly established grave of Cut Nose was reopened and the piece of skin was ceremoniously buried with the skull. These two pieces of Cut Nose are the only remains ever discovered of the thirty-eight Indians who were hanged.

Chapter Eleven

ॐ ✦ ॐ

Monumental Controversies

AFTER THE HANGING, the process of ridding the countryside of Indians continued. Hatred of the Indians persisted for many decades. The Dakotah Indians were thoroughly evicted from the State of Minnesota with only a few exceptions. The exceptions were some of the Dakotah who had been heroes on the side of the whites during the war. Many had served as scouts for the soldiers and some of the "friendlies" were responsible for rescuing many white people from being massacred. John Otherday was lauded as a hero for his actions during the war and was actually given an award of $2,500 by the government for his heroism. That was a very large sum of money in those days, more than enough to pay the full cost of a good-sized farm, for example.

All of those who had been found guilty of participating in the war but were not hanged spent the winter in the jail at Mankato. They were kept in irons, and their treatment was harsh. Thirteen of them died in that jail during that winter. In the spring, the survivors were sent to prison at Davenport, Iowa, where they served three years and then were set free.

The seventeen hundred men, women, and children who survived the march from the Lower Sioux Agency to Fort Snelling in November spent the winter there in a cramped compound with just enough sustenance to avoid starvation. Conditions were poor, and hundreds died during their internment. Fifteen hundred were transported to Nebraska in the spring for permanent placement there. They were shipped like animals in riverboats and again were abused along the way.

Then a hundred years passed. During that time, many of the Indians in Nebraska abandoned that place because it was not very desirable as a place to try to eke out a living. They went north to the Dakotas and gradually filtered back to their old haunts in Minnesota. But they avoided New Ulm and Mankato completely. As recently as 1990, I have personally heard Indians at the powwow in Mankato talking (as they are apt to do at a powwow) about "the old days" and how they would go out of their way to avoid passing through Mankato and New Ulm when traveling. Or else, they said, they would pass through these towns quickly, without stopping, at night. It was as if they thought that the history of the towns was evil and the people of the towns also were evil. They were certain that they were not safe there.

The Indians certainly have had good reason to think so. A number of incidents took place after the hanging of the thirty-eight that would serve to reinforce such thoughts.

After the exile of the Indians, there was a bounty on at least some of them. Six months after the hanging, an incident took place in which Chief Little Crow was shot dead, apparently for the bounty.[19] Chief Little Crow and his son had surreptitiously returned to Minnesota from Canada with a small band of Indians on a horse-stealing foray. On July 3, 1863, he and the boy were alone, picking wild berries in a field northwest of Hutchinson, Minnesota, when a passing farmer and the farmer's son spotted them. The farmer shot at Little Crow without warning, hitting him in the groin and then mortally wounding him with a second shot. Little Crow fired back and wounded the man who had shot him. The farmer's son ran off to get help. When the help arrived, they found Little Crow's body, but Little Crow's son had escaped. The farmer who shot Little Crow was also gone.

Little Crow's body was taken to Hutchinson. The farmer who had done the killing was there. He was only slightly wounded. He took Little Crow's scalp, leaving very little hair on the head. He wanted the scalp to

Little Crow. (Courtesy of the Blue Earth County Historical Society)

qualify for the seventy-five-dollar bounty offered by the State on Minnesota for killing hostile Indians. Some people remarked that the corpse looked like Chief Little Crow, but nobody knew (yet) that this was, indeed, the body of Little Crow. In this case, being Indian and picking wild berries appeared to have been enough hostility to qualify as a "hostile Indian." The body was laid out in the middle of Main Street where it suffered more mutilation. Young boys celebrating the Fourth of July holiday set off firecrackers in Little Crow's nostrils and ears. Finally, the body was thrown into a pile of refuse in the town dump. Nearly four weeks later, when Little Crow's son was captured, and he asked what happened to his father, the chief's body was retrieved from the dump and positively identified as that of Little Crow. The body was then subjected to further abuse including dismemberment. An Army officer, who helped retrieve the body, cut off Little Crow's head with his saber. Parts of the body were already missing. A local doctor took the head to preserve it for who knows what reason. Later on, more of the remains were salvaged.

In 1864, the man who killed Little Crow was given an award of $500 for having done the killing. Some of Little Crow's bones, including his skull, and his scalp were kept on display at the Minnesota Historical Society in St Paul for many years and were finally given to his family in 1971. Then, more than a hundred years after his death, he was given a dignified burial in Flandreau, South Dakota.

Another incident took place in New Ulm on Christmas Day in 1866, almost exactly four years after the hanging of the thirty-eight. Two trappers from Mankato were drinking in a New Ulm bar. They were not Indians but were dressed a lot like Indians, wearing buckskins and toting big knives as all trappers do. They got drunk, as did the other patrons in the bar. Eventually, most likely because of their clothing, they were enticed to dance like Indians. Soon they were fighting with the locals, perhaps playfully at first, but one of the good citizens from New Ulm was stabbed in the leg. The stabbing was probably an accident, but the man soon died from his wound. This led to both of the trappers being severely clobbered by the locals, one of them beaten to death. The other was near death when both of the trappers were lynched, hanged by the neck from the windows of the local jail. The death of the one still living was ensured when one citizen stabbed him a dozen times while he was still dangling on the rope.

During the night the bodies disappeared. When news of the lynching reached Mankato, a group of men from Mankato came to New Ulm to retrieve the bodies of their two respected citizens, but no one in New Ulm could or would say where the bodies were located. Their investigation ultimately determined that the bodies had been dismembered and dumped into the Minnesota River through a hole in the ice. Nevertheless, the party from Mankato managed to retrieve many of the body parts.

Bringing the killers in this case to justice was a very difficult task and probably was never actually achieved. There were some indictments, but at least two changes of venue were necessary, as it was evident that a fair trial was not possible to obtain in New Ulm. No jury selected there would convict the culprits. The trial ultimately took place twenty-five miles away in St Peter. In the end, only the man who stabbed the hanging trapper was convicted. He was sentenced to hang, but, because of technicalities, his sentence was reduced to ten years in prison.

Animosity toward Indians continued to be evident in the Mankato –New Ulm area for many, many years. For example, in 1912 a granite monument was placed on the location of the hanging of the thirty-eight in Mankato. It was much like a tombstone, about four feet high, three feet wide, and about a foot thick, set upright upon another piece of granite about the same size lying flat on the ground. This monument was designed to be neither positive nor negative in its message. It was not intended to honor the Indians who were hanged, nor was it intended to be any kind of boast about having hanged them. It was merely a statement of fact. The inscription on the marker read:

HERE
WERE HANGED
38
SIOUX INDIANS
DECEMBER 26th 1862

Memorial stone in Mankato, Minnesota. (Courtesy of the Blue Earth County Historical Society)

One would think that this marker would not be cause for or engender much protest, but it did rankle quite a few people, apparently. Some thought it was honoring the thirty-eight Indians who were hanged. It stimulated such questions as, "Why should they be honored?" and "What did they

116

do that was honorable?" and "Shouldn't we honor instead the hundreds of settlers they killed?"

That simple marker, as neutral in its message as it was, was the object of much controversy and even much abuse. The marker was sometimes vandalized by having red paint thrown on it. It looked gory when it was splashed with red paint. A local newspaper editor, Ken Berg, wrote many editorials protesting the recognition given to the Indians while their victims, the slain settlers, were relatively forgotten. The monument, together with the editorials, seemed to refresh the long-standing antagonism between the whites and the Indians. The Indians continued to stay away from the Mankato and New Ulm communities and would go out of their way to avoid the area when traveling through southern Minnesota.

To make matters worse, the proprietor of a local gas station got a lot of attention by stringing a cable in a high square around the perimeter of the station and hanging thirty-eight bald tires (popularly called "skins") on the cable. The gas station was located very close to where the actual hanging had taken place. This happened right at the end of World War II, when there were a lot of very bald tires. People had been driving on tires with absolutely no tread left on them. Tires had been in very short supply and had been rationed during the war. There were nine or ten "skins" hung on each side of the cable "scaffold" that surrounded the gas station, each tire suspended by a rope with a hangman's noose, and all the tires were painted red—"red skins." To make sure that people got the point, a large banner was displayed announcing, "38 RED SKINS BITE THE DUST!"

It took awhile for the more levelheaded people of the community to persuade the proprietor that this was in very bad taste. In fact, he probably wasn't persuaded. There were not very many people who protested this distasteful and insulting advertising, and instead it is likely that many were highly amused by it. But after a while the ad campaign just more or less died from disinterest, and the whole thing was removed. Even the gas station has been gone for many years.

It wasn't until the early 1970s that effective efforts were initiated to reduce the friction between the Indians and the whites. It seems that this task was just waiting for the ministrations of Amos Owen, a widely respected spiritual leader of many of the Dakotah in Minnesota at the time. A Mankato businessman, Bud Lawrence, had met Amos's brother-in-law, Wally Wells, casually while fishing near the Prairie Island Indian reservation where Amos lived. They had a long talk. Wally Wells suggested that Bud should go visit Amos, and he did that, without being introduced and unannounced, and he found Amos to be very receptive.

This union was apparently meant to be, although the two men were extremely different in their backgrounds and life experiences. Amos grew up a poor Indian boy on reservations. Bud grew up in a middle class white family. Amos was quite a worldly fellow as he grew up, served in the Army for five years in World War II, was severely wounded in the Philippines, and struggled with alcohol for a period of time after the war. Bud was quite straight-laced, a respected leader in the business community, and he had never been a drinker. Amos carved peace pipes even when he was just a boy. That activity guided him into the spiritualism of the Dakotah. His life then took a new tack so that he gradually became a spiritual leader, widely known and highly respected throughout the Dakotah Nation.

A close friendship developed between Amos and Bud. It lasted for decades. In fact, this friendship lasted for all the rest of Amos's life. They talked about the resentments that still existed between the Indians and the whites and how foolish it was for both sides to continue to carry grudges over things that happened a hundred years before. They decided to do something about it. They recruited others, especially Jim Buckley and the "Y's men" (YMCA), to join with them to initiate and organize a "reconciliation" effort to improve the relationships between Indians and whites in the Mankato–New Ulm area.

The first powwow took place in 1972. It was held in a Mankato ballpark. It was a simple affair, starting with a single Indian drum group and a relatively small number of notices sent out to Indian communities and various individuals, letting them know about the event and asking them to come and dance. There were no prizes to be given out, no special ceremonies to be held, except for one—that ceremony would be a prayer by Amos Owen to

Left to right: Bud Lawrence, Amos Owen, and Jim Buckley. These men conceived and promoted the first powwow in Mankato.

put an end to the hostilities that had continued between the whites and the Indians. That prayer largely succeeded.

That whole powwow succeeded wonderfully. There had been a lot of concern right up to the day of the powwow about whether anyone would actually come. Amos Owen repeatedly assured everyone that if preparations were made for a powwow, and if everything was right in the hearts of those making the preparations, then, "The people will come." When the day of the powwow arrived, a few people showed up at first, then many more, until there were people from all over the State of Minnesota and even more distant places arriving. More drum groups arrived representing many distant Indian communities. It was estimated that approximately one thousand Indians and as many local spectators attended that powwow. This powwow has become an annual event that takes place in Mankato every September.

The most recent powwows have had fifteen or more drums show up representing that many Indian communities. More than four hundred Native American dancers perform in colorful Indian regalia. There are varieties of Indian dances and beaded buckskins, feathered bustles and headdresses, and other traditional Native American paraphernalia are the order of the day. As many as four thousand spectators from local communities come to the powwow to watch the dancing and other various activities. There are vendors of Native American food and goods. Some spectators even become participants, camping for several days at the powwow, and even joining the Indians in the dancing. There are naming ceremonies, honor ceremonies, giveaways, contests, and some people even get married at the powwow. Each year, one afternoon is devoted to an educational program for hundreds of children who are bussed there from local schools.

Cut Nose comes to the powwow every year along with the other thirty-seven who were hanged in 1862. Each year there is a special ceremony in which the spirits of the thirty-eight hanged are "called in." There is evidence that these spirits do come and are present at the powwow. If you look for Cut Nose you may find him there. He is there. Do not be afraid of him because he will not harm you. Nor will any of the others—there are many spirits at the powwow. They do not come to do harm, but merely to be recognized. They are not evil. They do not purposely frighten anyone, though some people may be startled by them when they make their presence known. Many people at the powwow become aware of them. All who come to the powwow are welcome.

In addition to the annual powwow, there has been an annual Commemorative Run from Fort Snelling to the Mankato park where the powwow is held. This takes place every December 26, the anniversary date of the hanging of the thirty-eight. The runners start out at Fort Snelling at midnight and relay an eagle-feather staff a distance of about sixty miles through the night, often in extremely cold temperatures, arriving at Mankato in the morning at about the same time the Indians were hanged. Then a memorial service is held for the thirty-eight who were hanged. This ceremony is followed by a traditional Indian style feast which is available to all participants and spectators free of charge.

Helping to facilitate the annual powwow in September and the Memorial Run on December 26 is a local group of volunteers who do a lot of the groundwork for these events. This group is called the Mdewakanton Association. Most of the association members are local white folks. They work hard to help organize these and other events in cooperation with an advisory committee of Indian representatives from the various Indian communities in Minnesota. The association's purpose, however, is much broader than just facilitating these events. In the broadest terms, the purpose of the association is to improve the relationships between the white and Indian communities, just as Amos Owen desired. Amos Owen died in 1990, but his spirit is always present at the annual reconciliation powwow he helped to initiate in Mankato. It is still held the third weekend of September every year.

Not long before that first powwow in 1972, the stone monument on the site of the hanging of the thirty-eight was removed. It was buried in a place that not too many people know about anymore, although there was an article in the local newspaper that disclosed the location of the burial site at that time. That monument is buried in the memories of most people, also, and it is rarely mentioned by anyone anymore. That would have pleased Clarence Darrow, the lawyer famous for the "Scopes" trial, who is reported to have expressed disgust at seeing the monument during a visit to Mankato. After viewing the marker, he was reported by the *Mankato Free Press*, on December 27, 1937, to have said, "I can't make myself believe that the people of a civilized community would want to commemorate such an atrocious crime. I would never believe it if I didn't see the marker with my own eyes." It is not clear that he even knew about the subsequent grave robbery. The hanging alone appears to have been the "atrocious crime" that evoked his revulsion.

In November 1975, a "memorial reconciliation ceremony" was held on a site near where the hotly contested hanging marker had been. The Native Americans and the Mankato community co-sponsored the ceremony "in an effort to move forward together as one people striving for social change and equality through education and understanding."

The following text is taken directly from the new marker that was subsequently installed on this site in 1976. The Minnesota Historical Society and the Blue Earth County Historical Society erected the new marker. It has a large plaque that displays the following message:

DAKOTAH (SIOUX) MEMORIAL – 1862

The last act of Minnesota's Dakotah (Sioux) War took place here in Mankato on December 26, 1862, when thirty-eight Dakotah Indians died in a mass execution on this site.

The Dakotah War was a culmination of years of friction between Dakotah and white as settlement pushed into Indian hunting grounds. Government agents and missionaries hoped the Dakotah could be taught to live as farmers and worship as Christians, but, as Chief Big Eagle said many years later, "It seemed too sudden to make such a change. . . . If the Indians had tried to make the whites live like them, the whites would have resisted, and it was the same way with many Indians." The Minnesota uprising was one of the nation's most costly wars, both in lives lost and property destroyed. It resulted in the near depopulation of the frontier and the exile of the Dakotah from Minnesota.

At the war's conclusion, a five-man military commission held trials for several hundred Indian prisoners, and on November 5, 1862, 303 were condemned to death. Henry B. Whipple, Episcopal bishop of Minnesota, talked with President Abraham Lincoln on behalf of the Indians. After listening to the bishop and personally reviewing the trial records, Lincoln commuted the death sentences of all but thirty-eight prisoners. At 10 a.m. on December 26, 1862, the condemned men, chanting the Dakotah death song, marched in single file to a scaffold guarded by 1,400 troops in full battle dress. A crowd of citizens was on hand to witness the largest mass execution in United States history.

One can only speculate about how Clarence Darrow might have perceived this marker, but it's a good bet that he wouldn't have liked it any better than the old one. Still, almost thirty years have passed since it was installed, and nobody has vandalized or thrown red paint on it—yet.

Now there are additional targets for any aspiring vandals. A statue of a Sioux warrior dressed in winter clothing was completed and dedicated to honor the thirty-eight hanged. It is located within twenty feet of the memorial plaque. The dedication ceremony took place in 1987 on the anniversary date of the hanging, December 26, in connection with the annual Memorial Run.

More recently, a large buffalo was carved at the site of the hanging. In a ceremony on September 21, 1997, it was dedicated to commemorate the thirty-eight. The whole assemblage, the plaque, the Winter Warrior, and the buffalo, is part of what has now been established as the Amos Owen Parkette, sometimes called Reconciliation Park.

Frequently, there continue to be various references to "honoring" the thirty-eight Indians who were hanged in 1862 in Mankato. At many of the ceremonies at the annual Wacipi (powwow or dance) in September there is a lot of talk about honoring the thirty-eight. The annual run from Fort Snelling to Land of Memories Park on December 26th, the anniversary of the execution, is an event that is established for the express purpose of honoring the thirty-eight Indians who were hanged. Some of the members of the Association that facilitates these events talk unhesitatingly about honoring the thirty-eight, but some talk about these events as "Commemorative" events, or "Memorial" events. Some members are reluctant to say that these events are held to "honor" the thirty-eight, and they might have good reason to be disinclined to do that.

Why would we "honor" the Indians who were hanged? Are they to be honored because they were hanged? Probably not because that's not much of an accomplishment. Are they honored for being found guilty of participating in the uprising? Maybe some of them might be honored for their actions, but not all. In their trials, most didn't face their captors patriotically, like Indian patriots. No, instead they denied the charges leveled against them. Most said they didn't fight, much less kill anyone. Yet, estimates of the number of settlers killed in the 1862 Uprising range from four hundred to eight hundred. A great deal of killing did happen, and more than a few men were responsible. Few of the accused acted in their trials as if they were proud of what they had done, if they admitted it at all, according to eyewitness accounts and the handwritten transcripts of their trials. In actuality, there were some heroes among the thirty-eight, but there was little heroic pride or defiance displayed by the Indians.

The trials were a farce, and it would be interesting to see what would be the result of a retrial today on the basis of available information. The authority to conduct such trials was highly questionable in the first place.

Most of those who were convicted of "participating in the uprising" were convicted on the basis of hearsay evidence. They were sentenced to death merely for having been on the other (losing) side in the uprising. Imagine what would have happened if the Nuremberg trials following World War II had sentenced to death all the soldiers of the other (Axis) side who merely "participated" in the war.

Would we honor the thirty-eight for what they were accused of having done? For killing settlers, old men, women, and children? For mutilating their bodies? Not likely, even if we understood completely the cultural influences that could have caused the Indian warriors to do the things they did. For example, we know about the Indian belief that, after killing an enemy, eating his heart might confer the strength of the enemy. Castrating the enemy's body was believed to prevent the enemy from having children in the next life. Cutting off his right arm would make certain that he would not strike a blow against Indians in the future life. Removal of a woman's breasts would ensure that she could not nurse her young in the afterlife. These Indian beliefs were the reasons for the mutilations.

Most of the white survivors of the uprising did not know about these beliefs or did not understand them. As a consequence, they were enraged by the horrors they found at country homesteads in the aftermath of the fighting. Many of the bodies of the settlers were incredibly mutilated. Nevertheless, the Indian warriors who committed these horrors were likely to have been acting righteously out of their cultural heritage, instead of doing these things as a result of malicious hatred and savagery as white folks believed.

Were old men, women, and children enemies of the Indians? Perhaps they were, at least from the point of view of the Indians. Young whites were seen as immature adults, who would become adult enemies if allowed to mature. Women could bear more white babies. Old men could shoot Indians as well as young men, and sometimes better. So, from the point of view of the Indians, they all had to go.

It is certainly true that the whites were guilty of creating a holocaust for the Indians after the uprising was over. There is no doubt that whites wanted to rid the countryside of all the Indians. Military records are replete with documented orders from the top to take no prisoners in any of the subsequent battles. The actions of the whites demonstrated that there was every intention of ending the existence of all the Indians completely, if not by killing them all, then by assimilating them into the white culture or by getting rid of them, sending them elsewhere. Every approach was tried, but none was successful.

There is clearly the possibility that the Indians were guilty of initiating a holocaust even before the whites did that, however, because it appears that they had the intention of ridding the countryside of all whites when the uprising began. If that was, indeed, their main purpose, their goal, then killing all whites, male or female, young or old, was the order of the day, the main thing on the agenda, the basis of the uprising, and those who did that were acting in the interests of their Nation, the Indian Nation. If they fought well, accomplished much, killed many of the enemy people, should they not be recognized and lauded (honored) for their exceptional performance of duty?

Do we not honor and romanticize Baron Manfred Von Richthofen, the "Red Knight," a German fighter pilot in World War I, for his heroic exploits in the downing of eighty Allied planes? Also known as "The Red Baron," he killed more of our allied airmen than any other fighter pilot. He killed our pilots, and he killed a lot of them. He did it well. We respect that. As a result, he has become exceedingly famous, and we look up to his memory. He has earned a place in our history books and on pizza commercials.

Think about more recent holocausts. How do we remember the horrors inflicted upon the Jews in the Nazi concentration camps? There are memorials to them at the sites of the mass graves in which their bodies (or ashes) are buried. But we do not honor the Nazis for killing the Jews. If there were a mass grave for the thirty-eight Indians who were hanged, would there be any objection to a memorial to them being erected at the site? Would there be objections to having their names listed on a stone there? Could they not be memorialized as victims of vengeful white retribution after the uprising ended?

Unfortunately, there is no grave for the thirty-eight. They were buried in a mass grave near the river on the day they were hanged, but then they suffered the additional indignity of having their grave robbed, all of the bodies taken from the grave less than twenty-four hours after the execution and burial. The bodies were to be used later as cadavers, or sold for that ignominious purpose, even without consideration of the rights or wishes of the next of kin. Therefore, there is no grave for the thirty-eight Indians who were executed. Even the precise location of what was the gravesite is no longer known by anyone. Doesn't this fact alone justify the placement of the names of the thirty-eight at the site of the execution?

At many Civil War battle sites, soldiers of both sides of the war are buried side by side. All of the fallen are given the same honors and respect by everyone who visits those sacred places. No, on second thought, there is evidence that blacks were buried prejudiciously in a cemetery of their own.

Without intending to imply that the Indians who participated in the uprising were really bad guys, isn't it true that there are headstones on the graves and memorials erected in memory of nearly all the really bad guys in history? Benedict Arnold is buried with his wife, and the grave is revered as a valued historical site. The grave of John Wilkes Booth is a tourist attraction, as are the graves of many really bad guys. You can pay your respects at the well-marked graves of:

Lee Harvey Oswald (Shannon Rose Hill Memorial Park, Fort Worth, Texas.)

Al Capone (Mount Carmel Cemetery, Hillside, Illinois.)

John Dillinger (Crown Hill Cemetery, Indianapolis, Indiana.)

Jesse James (Mount Olivet Cemetery, Kearney, Missouri.)

and celebrate "Jesse James Days" in Northfield, Minnesota, every September.

80 ♦ 03

THERE IS AN INTERESTING FOOTNOTE about Chief Ernest Wabasha, the present-day hereditary chief of the Mdewakanton Tribe. He is the acknowledged great-great-grandson of Chief Wabasha, who was one of the chiefs of the Mdewakanton Tribe at the time of the 1862 Sioux Uprising. It is a not-so-well-known fact that he is also a great-great-grandson of the notorious Jesse James. Ernie Wabasha, himself, told me that Jesse had taken refuge at an Indian camp while on the run and was given Indian hospitality overnight. The woman who kept Jesse warm that night was Chief Ernest Wabasha's great-great-grandmother. Chief Ernest Wabasha is a direct descendant of the offspring that resulted from that union. The chief has been invited to attend the Jesse James' descendants reunions in Kansas City. He has done that and has been accepted there as one of the direct descendants of Jesse James.

When it comes to honoring bad guys, it seems that our government, the United States Government, holds the track record. Twenty Congressional Medals of Honor, our country's highest award for bravery and valor in the field of combat, were awarded to U.S. Cavalry soldiers who massacred more than 200 (estimates range up to 375) Indian men, women, and children, most of whom were unarmed, at Wounded Knee, South Dakota, on December 29, 1890. There have been efforts on the part of many people to have the award of these medals rescinded, but all to no avail. In 1916, there was reconsideration given to all of the Medals of Honor that had ever been awarded. More than 900 were found that failed to meet the standards for bravery and valor and were rescinded, but the medals awarded at Wounded Knee made the cut and were not withdrawn.

It might be argued that the killing at Wounded Knee occurred after the Indians did their "dirty work" in Minnesota and after the Battle of the Little Big Horn, General Custer's "Last Stand." The massacre at Wounded Knee probably was vengeance for Custer's Last Stand. The motivations for the massacre at Wounded Knee—hatred, vengeance, ridding the territory of Indians—appear to be much less honorable than the motives of the Indians in the 1862 Uprising.

The motives of the Indians in 1862, by comparison, were honorable. The Indians had such motives as a wish to defend or regain their homeland and a desire to recover and maintain or continue their traditional ways of life. They wanted freedom from dependency on the white man and freedom from the tyranny of the white man. How reasonable is it to argue that the vengeful actions of those Seventh Cavalry soldiers were more honorable or heroic than the actions of the thirty-eight Indians who were hanged?

The Mdewakanton Association, which facilitates the powwow in September and the Commemorative Run on December 26, has, as part of its purpose, the promotion and preservation of the culture of the American Indian and encouraging cultural exchange with others. The association has no policy regarding the "honoring" of the thirty-eight Indians who were hanged. Individual members might honor the thirty-eight if they choose to do so. Some members might do that because they are direct descendants of one or more of the thirty-eight. Others might honor the thirty-eight for other reasons. A majority of the members of the association are not Indians. Each member has the individual freedom to choose to honor the thirty-eight or to have any other attitude as an individual choice for which the member will be individually responsible.

As a final note, I will observe that all of the thirty-eight who were hanged died bravely. They represented an outstanding sampling of men who rose up to be counted on behalf of their people. They were men who could not tolerate having the very existence of their people stolen from them through lies, politics, and force while the people were desperately cold, sick, hungry, and frightened. These men must be respected for that.

Cut Nose stood out among the thirty-eight as a leader who never gave up, even at the very end. He recognized that the old ways of the Dakotah people were something of value to be maintained and not abandoned. He was a model for many contemporary Native Americans who strive to teach their children Native American languages and traditional Native American culture. History owes Cut Nose a great deal more attention and recognition than he has been given.

Epilogue

HE SAGA OF CUT NOSE and his compatriots is not yet complete. The search goes on for more of the remains of Cut Nose and the remains of the rest of the thirty-eight who were hanged. When one of the skulls submitted to Hamline University was identified as that of Cut Nose, the question of what happened to the rest of his skeleton arose. It is well known that Mayo Clinic had the entire skeleton of Cut Nose at one point, so what did the clinic do with the rest of the skeleton? They must have some explanation of what was done with it or produce it, one or the other. Currently, there is an effort to initiate some negotiation with the Mayo Clinic to get their response to this question.

The original memorial stone commemorating the hanging of the thirty-eight in 1862 has disappeared. The city of Mankato had it removed before the first reconciliation powwow in 1972. Apparently, however, there is still some controversy over it, even in its absence. A recent article in the *Mankato Free Press* reported that, since the monument was removed, much speculation has developed over what was done with it. The writer added, "What happened to the marker and where it might be today have become a thing of legend." One report had it buried under a city sand pile. But there are other rumors about its location, including "some city worker's backyard or shed," or "crushed up and put under the buffalo statue," and some people claim to have seen it "by a cabin somewhere."

Jessica Potter, director of the local historical society, expressed ambivalence about the monument. She was reported to have said, "For what it represents, that's where I'm happy it's lost," but she also said that for the sake of history, "If someone came forward with it, we'd be happy to accept it." Obviously, somebody knows where this stone is located, but the fact that nobody comes forward with the information is proof that it remains a very sensitive issue.

After the hangings, seventeen hundred Mdewakanton Sioux were forcibly relocated from Minnesota to Fort Snelling where two hundred died from starvation and exposure during a winter of suffering. From there they were moved to Nebraska for resettlement. While they were in Nebraska, many more of them died for the same reasons as during the first year. Later, the State of Minnesota passed a law giving land grants to Mdewakanton Sioux Indians who were still residing in Minnesota at the time the law was enacted. These were Sioux Indians who hid out and thereby avoided being relocated. They are now calling themselves the "loyalists."

Subsequently, many of the Indians who had been relocated filtered back into Minnesota and eventually established very lucrative casinos on Indian lands and were very selective as to who would be allowed membership on the Indian reservations (probably to limit the distribution of income from the casinos). There were many loyalists who were not enrolled on reservations and who were then denied membership when they applied for it.

The loyalists are now not only engaged in litigation to gain membership, but also claiming that many of the Indians who have membership are themselves unqualified. The loyalists claim that those who were deported lost their qualifications as Mdewakantons by virtue of having been relocated to other tribes of Indians in Nebraska and South Dakota. Their claims have found some support in a federal court and are being taken seriously. The final result of this controversy is yet to be determined.

∽ ◆ ∾

Notes

The following are footnotes on selected expressions found in the text of this book.
The notes are merely elaborations, clarifications, or explanations that might help to
make the selected expressions less questionable or less contestable, or more under-
standable. Those considerations provided the basis for making the selections.

[1]This is a well-documented fact recorded in several places, but most
convincingly acknowledged in the autobiography of Charles Mayo, one of
the famous Mayo brothers.

[2]The Ojibwa Indians called the Dakotah "Nadowessioux," which was
an Ojibwa word that meant "little snakes." French traders shortened this
expression to "Sioux" which is now so commonly used as a name for the
Dakotah that it now is accepted even among the Dakotah, although
"Dakotah" is preferred. "Dakotah" means "friends" or "allies" (War Cloud,
p. x). Sometimes the meaning of "Dakotah" is said to be "balanced and in
harmony." It is easy to understand, therefore, how "Dakotah" might be preferred over "Sioux."

[3]After the war ended, Sarah Wakefield told a story relevant to this.
She had been held captive during the whole duration of the conflict, protected by Chaska and his mother from being slaughtered by the Indians.

She told of an occasion when Chaska's grandfather hid Sarah and her infant daughter in a haystack to prevent them from being murdered by rampaging Indian warriors who were intent upon killing all whites and even half-breeds. When Sarah heard noises near her hiding place, she choked her little girl to keep the girl from making any noise that would give away their position. "I clasped my hands around her throat until she was black in the face, for I knew her cries would lead to our discovery and death," she said. She didn't kill the girl, but merely kept her quiet. She might well have learned to do this from listening to stories told by her captors. In any case, this behavior, as cruel as it seems at first blush, is easily understandable, given the circumstances in which it occurred, and it saved the lives of both the mother and the child.

[4]On September 14, 1838, Nicollet set out on an expedition to explore what is now an eight county area of southern Minnesota (Blue Earth, Dakota, Faribault, Jackson, LeSueur, Martin, Rice, and Waseca counties) that he named the Undine Region. With him were at least nine others, including several Indian guides, Nez Coupee, or Cut Nose, among them (Bray and Bray, p. 121).

In a letter to Henry Sibley dated July 24, 1838 (but probably misdated and written September 24, 1838) Nicollet wrote (Bray and Bray, p.227):

> MY DEAR FRIEND –
> I send back my guide, the Cut Nose. Be kind enough to furnish him some goods of his own selection to the amount of $10, which you will charge to the account of the expedition under my control, under the authority of the United States.
> I send back the Cut Nose because last night he gave me his word which he did not keep this morning, and as the Indians do not hesitate to take one another's part on such occasions, you see I do not hesitate.
> We advance our little train always with success, caring nothing for rain or cold. We expect to arrive at Spirit Lake after to-morrow.
> Adieu, good friend.
> Yours, with all my soul,
> J.N. Nicollet

In a footnote (number 21), at the bottom of the same page, it is noted that Cut Nose subsequently (in November, 1838) was paid the ten dollars for his services as guide.

[5]The peak number of buffaloes on the western prairies was estimated to be near fifty million. The buffaloes were extremely important to the Indians all across the western plains. The Indians hunted them for their sustenance and were good stewards of the immense herd. They slaughtered only the number they needed and used every part of the buffalo for one purpose or another; the meat was eaten, the bones made soup, the hide made robes, clothing, and fabric for other purposes. Almost nothing was wasted.

White men, however, wasted the buffaloes ruthlessly. "Buffalo Skinners" hunted them for the hides and the tongues, which were a delicacy in New York, leaving the carcasses to rot in the sun. When the railroads were established across the plains, trainloads of white men would shoot at herds of buffalo just for sport, killing as many as they could and wasting entirely all that they killed. This practice was condoned and even promoted by the government in an overt effort to exterminate buffaloes and thereby eliminate the Indians. This effort nearly succeeded as the number of buffaloes was reduced from near fifty million to fewer than 500. The buffaloes came that close to becoming extinct.

[6]"A sense of betrayal set in among many young Dakota men. The loss of their life ways and hunting grounds and the large and continual influx of whites from Europe and the East created a sense of defeat, cynicism, and anger, all of which served as a backdrop to the war. Dakotas who had converted to Christianity and become farmers—"cut hairs"—were favored by new policies, given more money, and were better able to feed their families." (Wakefield, p. 19)

[7]All of this is a true story according to Samuel J. Brown, son of the Dakotah woman whose raucous objections saved this party of people. He witnessed the event and recounted it (Anderson and Woodworth, pp. 74-76). He added a poignant detail about the incident when the white men ran away. After starting to run, one of them returned to the wagon to get his boots. He picked up one boot, started to run again, and then returned a sec-

ond time for the other boot. Running off again with the Indians threatening to shoot him, he returned a third time, this time to embrace the young woman whom he had recently married and whom Cut Nose was now leading away from the wagon so that he could take his pleasure with her. The man ran up to her, saying, "Shoot me, but I shall first kiss my wife." He embraced her and smothered her with kisses while the Indians stood by, "paralyzed" by his brazen actions. Then he did run away, with Cut Nose again threatening to shoot him.

[8]President Lincoln received a letter (reproduced below) jointly written by a Minnesota Senator and two Congressional Representatives from Minnesota. Access to a photostatic copy of the hand written letter is available at the Reference Library of the Minnesota Historical Society in St Paul, Minnesota in the last box of the trial transcripts. The letter, replete with exaggerations and derogatory descriptions of Indians, clearly demonstrates the extreme attitudes that were held regarding these executions and the Indians generally:

> To the President of the United States,
> Sir:
> We have learned, incidentally, that you intend to pardon or reprieve a large majority of the Indians in Minnesota, who have been formally condemned for their participation in the brutal massacres of our people, in the months of August and September last.
> If this is your purpose, as Representatives from that State, we beg leave Most respectfully to protest against it, and we do so for the following reasons:
> These Indians were condemned, most of them, upon the testimony of women whom they had carried into captivity, after having murdered their fathers, husbands, and brothers, and who were treated by these Indians with a brutality never known in this country, or equaled in the practice of the most barbarous nations.
> There were nearly ninety female captives. They were the wives and daughters of our neighbors and friends. They were intelligent and virtuous women; some of them were wives and mothers, others were young and interesting girls.
> These savages, to whom you purpose to extend your Executive clemency, when the whole country was quiet, and the farmers were busi-

ly engaged in gathering their crops, arose with fearful violence, and, traveling from one farmhouse to another, indiscriminately murdered all the men, boys, and little children they came to; and although they sometimes spared the lives of the mothers and daughters, they did so only to take them into a captivity which was infinitely worse than death.

Mr. President, let us relate to you some facts with which we fear you have not heretofore been made acquainted:

These Indians whom (as we understand) you propose to pardon and set free, have murdered in cold blood nearly, or quite, one thousand of our people, savaged our frontier for a distance of more than one hundred and fifty miles north and south, burned the houses of the settlers, and driven from their houses more than ten thousand of our people. They seized and carried into captivity nearly one hundred women and young girls, and in nearly every instance treated them with the most fiendish brutality.

To show you, sir, the enormity of these outrages, we beg leave to state a few facts, which are well known to our people, but delicacy forbids that we should mention the names of the parties to whom we refer.

In one instance some ten or twelve of these Indians visited the house of a worthy farmer, who, at the time, was engaged with his sons in stacking wheat. They stealthily approached the fence where this honest farmer was at work, and, seizing their opportunity, shot the father and his two sons at the stack. They then went to the house, killed two little children in the presence of their mother, who was quite ill of consumption, and then, they took the sick mother and a beautiful little daughter, thirteen years of age, into captivity.

But this is not all, nor is it the most appalling feature of this awful tragedy.

Its horror is yet to be revealed. After removing these unhappy prisoners to a lodge which was some miles away, these fiends incarnate, placing a guard over the body of the weary and exhausted mother, took her little girl outside of the lodge, removed all her clothes, and fastened her upon her back on the ground. Then they commenced their work of brutality upon the body of this young girl. One by one, they violated her person, unmoved by her cries and unchecked by the evident signs of her approaching dissolution. This work was continued until her Heavenly Father relieved her from her suffering.

They left her dead upon the Ground.

This outrage was committed within a few feet of a sick and dying mother.

There is another instance, of a girl, eighteen years of age. We knew her well before and at the time of her capture. She was as refined and beautiful girl as we had in the State. None had more or better friends; no one was more worthy of them than she. She was taken; her arms were tied behind her; she was made fast to the ground, and ravished by some eight or ten of these convicts, before the cords were unloosed from her limbs. This girl fortunately lived to testify against the wretches who had thus violated her.

Without being more specific we will state that all or nearly all the women who were captured were violated in this way. Again, there was a little boy brought to St Paul, whose father and mother had been murdered, whose life was spared, as a witness of the horrid nature of this massacre.

His right eye was cut completely Out; it had fallen from its socket and perished on his cheek. His two little sisters, aged respectively six and four years, were also saved, but in an awfully mutilated condition; their tender arms mangled with the savages' knives, and otherwise fearfully wounded, and left on the ground for dead.

Mr. President:

There was no justification, Or pretext, even, for these brutalities. We state what we know when We say that the Sioux Agent, Major Galbraith, has labored faithfully and Efficiently for the welfare of these Indians.

The government, as you know, has built a house and opened a farm for every one of these Indians who would reside upon and cultivate it. Missionaries, as our worthy Bishop can testify, have labored zealously Among them for their spiritual welfare.

There has been paid to them yearly the interest upon two millions of dollars. Farming implements have been purchased, and farmers have been employed by the Government to improve and cultivate their lands.

These Indians are called, by some, prisoners of war. There was no war about it. It was wholesale robbery, rape, murder. These Indians were not at war with their murdered victims.

The people of Minnesota, Mr. President, have stood firm by you and by your administration. They have given both you and it their cordial support. They have not violated the law. They have borne these sufferings with a patience such as but few people ever exhibited under such extreme trial. These Indians are now at their mercy; but our people have not risen up to slaughter them, because they believed that their President would deal with them justly.

We are told, Mr. President, that a committee from Pennsylvania, whose families are living happily in their pleasant homes in that State, have called upon you and petitioned you to pardon these Indians. We have a high respect for the religious sentiments of your petitioners; but we submit it that it is in bad taste; indeed, that it is entirely unbecoming them to interfere in matters with which they are so little acquainted, and which relate to the security of our own people.

We protest against it, because, if the President does not permit these executions to take place under the forms of law, the outraged people of Minnesota will dispose of these wretches without law. These two peoples cannot live together. We do not wish to see mob law inaugurated in Minnesota, as it certainly will be, if you force the people to it.

We tremble at the approach of such a condition of things in our State.

You can give us peace, or you can give us lawless violence. We pray you, sir, in view of all that we have suffered, and of the danger which still awaits us—let the Law be executed; let justice be done our People.

> With high respect,
> We are, Sir,
> Your obedient Servants,
> M.S. Wilkinson
> Cyrus Aldrich
> Wm. Windom

[9]The names are spelled phonetically exactly as they were in the list that was hand written by Abraham Lincoln.

The text of President Lincoln's letter (A photostatic copy of this letter also is at the Minnesota Historical Society in St Paul):

Executive Mansion,
Washington, December 6th, 1862
Brigadier General H. H. Sibley
St Paul, Minnesota
Ordered, that of The Indians and Half-breeds sentenced to be hanged by the Military Commission, composed of Colonel Brooks, Lt. Colonel Marshall, Captain Grant, Captain Bailey, and Lieutenant Olin, and lately sitting in Minnesota, you cause to be executed, on Friday, the nineteenth day of December, instant, the following named, to wit:

"Te-he-hdo-ne-cha," No. 2 by the record.
"Tazoo," alias "Plan-doo-ta," No. 4 by the record.
"Wy-a-the-to-wah," No. 5 by the record.
"Hin-han-shoon-ko-yag," No. 6 by the record.
"Muz-za-bom-a-du," No. 10 by the record.
"Wah-pay-du-ta," No. 11 by the record.
"Wa-he-hua," No. 12 by the record.

"Qua-ma-ni," No. 14 by the record.

"Ta-te-mi-ma," No. 15 by the record.

"Rda-in-yan-kua," No. 19 by the record.

"Do-wan-sa," No. 22 by the record.

"Ha-pan," No. 24 by the record.

"Shoon-ka-ska" (White Dog), No. 35 by the record.

"Toon-kan-e-chah-tah-mane," No. 67 by the record.

"E-tay-hoo-tay,"   No. 68 by the record.

"Am-da-cha," No. 69 by the record.

"Hay-pee-don," or "Wamne-omne-ho-ta," No. 70 by the record.

"Mahpe-o-ke-na-ji," No. 96 by the record.

"Henry Milord," a Half-breed, No.115 by the record.

"Chaskay-don," or, Chaskay-etah," No.121 by the record.

"Baptist Campbell," a Half-breed, No.138 by the record.

"Tah-ta-kay-gay," No.155 by the record.

"Ha-pink-pa," No.170 by the record.

"Hypolite Auge,"a Half-breed, No.175 by the record.

"Na-pa-shue," No.178 by the record.

"Wa-kan-tan-ka," No.210 by the record.

"Toon-kan-ka-yag-e-na-jin," No.225 by the record.

"Ma-kat-e-na-jin," No.254 by the record.

"Pa-zee-koo-tay-ma-ni," No.264 by the record.

"Ta-ta-hde-don," No.279 by the record.

"Wa-she-choon," or, "Toon-kan-shkan-shkan-mene-hay," No.318 by
the record.

"A-e-cha-ga," No.327 by the record.

"Ha-tan-inkoo,"   No.333 by the record.

"Chay-ton-hoon-ka," No.342 by the record.

"Chan-ka-had," No.359 by the record.

"Had-hin-hday," No.373 by the record.

"O-ya-tay-a-koo," No.377 by the record.

"May-hoo way-wa," No.382 by the record.

"Wa-kin-yan-na," No.383 by the record.

The other condemned prisoners you will hold, subject to further orders, taking care that they neither escape, nor are subjected to any unlawful violence.

Abraham Lincoln,
President of the United States

138

[10]The text of this letter is reproduced from Hughes, Thomas, History of Blue Earth County, p. 131

[11]After the hanging, one of the attending clergy (Reverend Riggs) wrote to Mrs. Wakefield:

> Dear Madam:—In regard to the mistake by which Chaska was hung instead of another, I doubt whether I can satisfactorily explain it. We all felt a solemn responsibility, and a fear that some mistake should occur. We had forgotten that he was condemned under the name of We-chan-hpe-wash-tay-do-pe. We knew he was called Chaska in the prison, and had forgotten that any other except Robert Hopkins, who lived by Dr. Williamson, was so called. We never thought of the third one; so when the name Chaska was called in the prison on that fateful morning, your protector answered to it and walked out. I do not think anyone was really to blame. We all regretted the mistake very much… (Wakefield, pp. 121-122).

[12]While it is true that one of the thirty-eight did fall to the ground after the rope broke, some will say that it was not Cut Nose. The soldiers did string the fallen Indian back up just as described, whoever it was. An article in the *Harper's Weekly* magazine named that Indian as Rattling Runner. However, in the History of Blue Earth County by Thomas Hughes, page 134, Cut Nose is said to have been the one whose rope broke.

[13]During the last years of the Civil War, men were being drafted into military service. Dr. Mayo was then employed as a medical examiner to determine whether applications for deferment from the draft were justified on the grounds of physical disability. He examined several hundred men in a day, and he acknowledged seeing some of them at his home after hours when he would charge a five dollar fee for his services, believing that there was nothing wrong with that. When he was accused of being corrupt, however, military authorities conducted an investigation of his activities and dismissed him from his duties as an examiner for the military. Nevertheless, public opinion remained firm that Dr. Mayo's integrity was unquestionable. (See Clapesattle, pp. 78-86)

[14]It is interesting that at one meeting of the Mdewakanton Association a rather angry and outspoken, well educated Dakotah woman was ventilat-

ing some of her anger over all of the 38 bodies having been stolen from the grave right after their burial. She said, "They didn't even give them time to cool off!" I explained to her that the purpose of removing the bodies from the grave immediately was precisely to cool them off and freeze them for preservation.

[15]In 1937, a newspaper reporter for the *Mankato Free Press* reviewed some old records and found that a Captain of Company K of the Minnesota Seventh Infantry claimed that when authorities heard that the Indian bodies had been dug up he was sent with a detachment of men to rebury any that were left on the ground. When he arrived at the site of the burial, he actually found some men of the Minnesota Tenth shooting at an Indian body tied to a tree. He ordered them to stop , but they disregarded his order and continued to shoot. He also claimed, "There were four or five [bodies] hidden under logs and brush. We buried them again, but by the end of the week I presume there was not an Indian left." (*Mankato Free Press*, January 25, 1937).

[16]It is an absolute fact that to this day nobody has ever found that gravesite again. Even today there is no gravesite identified as such in Mankato. Nobody knows specifically where it was. In the absence of that knowledge, the "Amos Owen Parkette" has been established near the site where the hanging actually took place.

[17]It is worth noting that in all of my review of relevant papers and documents, I was unable to determine the identity or final disposition of that single body. It might just have been thrown into the dump, like the body of Chief Little Crow was initially just thrown into the dump some six months later. That body was riddled with bullets. Most likely it was reburied near the tree where it had been tied up instead of being transported any distance. If so, the exact location of that grave also is not known.

[18]This is a well-known fact that is clearly documented in many places including Charles Mayo's autobiography.

[19]All of the details of Little Crow's death are quite well documented. (Anderson, pp. 7-8)

[20]The details of this incident are reported in a recent (2002) newspaper article (Murray).

Bibliography

Anderson, Gary C., *Little Crow: Spokesman for the Sioux*. Minnesota Historical Society Press, 1986, St Paul, Minnesota.

Anderson, Gary C., and Woolworth, Alan R., *Through Dakota Eyes: Narrative Accounts of the Minnesota Indian War of 1862*. Minnesota Historical Society Press, 1988, St Paul, Minnesota.

Bray, Edmund C. and Bray, Martha Coleman (Eds.), *Joseph N. Nicollet on the Plains and Prairies: The Expeditions of 1838-39: With Journals, Letters, and Notes on the Dakota Indians (translated from the French and Edited by Edmund C. Bray and Martha Coleman Bray)*. Minnesota Historical society Press, 1993, St Paul, Minnesota.

Carley, Kenneth, *The Sioux Uprising of 1862* (Second Edition), 1976, The Minnesota Historical Society, St Paul, Minnesota.

Clapesattle, Helen B. *The Doctors Mayo*. The University of Minnesota Press, 1941, Minneapolis, Minnesota.

Hughes, Thomas, *History of Blue Earth County*. Middle West Publishing Company, 1901(?), Chicago, Illinois.

Krohn, Tim, *Mankato Free Press*, December 4, 2005, p. E1.

Mankato Free Press, January 25, 1937, p. 7.

Mankato Free Press, December 23, 1937.

Mayo, Charles H., *Mayo: The Story of My Family and My Career.* Thomas, Springfield, Illinois, 1951.

Morris, Lucy Leavenworth Wilder, Ed., *Old Rail Fence Corners: Frontier Tales told by Minnesota Pioneers.* Minnesota Historical Society Press, 1976, St Paul, Minnesota.

U.S. Army Military Commission, Sioux War Trials, 1862, Minnesota Historical Society, St Paul, MN

Murray, R. A. "Sad Christmas Tale," *Mankato Free Press*, December 23, 2002.

Schultz, Duane, *Over the Earth I Come*, St. Martins Press, 1993.

Wakefield, Sarah F., *Six Weeks in the Sioux Tepees: A Narrative of Indian Captivity.* Argus Book and Job Printing Office, 1864, Shakopee, Minnesota.

Wakefield, Sarah F. *Six Weeks in the Sioux Tepees: a Narrative of Indian Captivity*, University of Oklahoma Press, 1997, Norman, Oklahoma.

War Cloud, Paul, *Dakotah Sioux Indian Dictionary*. Tekakwitha Fine Arts Center, 1989, Sisseton, South Dakota.

Index

.

ERRATA:.
p. 108 beginning of first paragraph:.
     Instead of "For me, Mr. Nelson's response".
    substitute: For me, Mr. [name omitted]'s response